THE
LEGACY PATH

Discover Intentional
Spiritual Parenting

BRIAN HAYNES

randall house
114 Bush Rd | Nashville, TN 37217 | randallhouse.com

The Legacy Path

WHAT OTHERS ARE SAYING ABOUT
THE LEGACY PATH

As the entire D6 movement has grown up in recent years, Brian Haynes has been a consistent voice of practical instruction for parents and leaders who are ready to begin the journey. *The Legacy Path* joins together the "hows" and the "whys" of godly parenting in a fresh and exciting way that I can't wait to share with our congregation. Intensely inspiring and profoundly biblical, this book will positively impact your family for generations to come.

Ryan Rush
Senior Pastor, Bannockburn Baptist Church

If you are looking for a way to lead your kids to have a lasting faith in Jesus Christ "so that they may enjoy long life" (Deut. 6) then I would strongly recommend *The Legacy Path* because it is simple, practical, and transformational. Through *The Legacy Path*, Brian Haynes has provided a great resource that will help families, of every shape and size, bring Christ and Christ-like living back into the center of their home.

Mark Holmen
Author, Pastor and Missionary to the Faith@Home Movement
Faithathome.com

The Legacy Path is written by my good friend Brian Haynes who has had a front row seat for years as a practitioner of youth and family ministry. Brian loves his Savior, his bride, his children, the church, the Gospel and the next generation! *The Legacy Path* is a great gift to the church and should be read by every parent. I cannot wait to get this book in the hands of our parents at Providence.

Steve Wright
Pastor of Family Discipleship
Providence Baptist Church
Author of *reThink* and *ApParent Privilege*

Parenting is not simply about raising kids. Parenting advances the Kingdom of Christ to the ends of the Earth! The Legacy Path brings this compelling biblical vision into every day family life. Writing from a deep love for God and His Word, Haynes will encourage and equip you to impact your family for generations to come.

Dr. Rob Rienow
Visionary Family Ministries
www.visionaryfam.com

The most effective strategy for reaching the generations with the Gospel requires that parents be intimately involved with the discipleship of their children. Brian Haynes has once again served the church, this time giving parents a biblical and workable strategy to carry out their primary responsibility. Every Christian parent should get this book and put it into practice. I commend it without reservation.

Randy Stinson, Ph.D.
Dean, School of Church Ministries
The Southern Baptist Theological Seminary
President, The Council on Biblical Manhood and Womanhood

DEDICATION

To Hailey, Madelyn, Eden, Micah, Mia, M'Kayla, Annah,
Noah, Eva, Evan, Benjamin
& the next generation.

To the parents of the boys who will marry my daughters…

SH'MA!

ACKNOWLEDGMENTS

In so many ways there would be no legacy path if it weren't for my wife and children. There certainly would be no book without them. Angela, thank you for your friendship and partnership as we walk the legacy path with our girls. I have known you since you were fifteen and you only grow more beautiful with each passing day. Thanks for sacrificing countless hours allowing me to take this message to the world. You have made the greater sacrifice. I love you. Hailey, thanks for your loving heart and your warrior spirit, which makes me a better Dad. Madelyn, thanks for your sensitivity and grace. Eden, thanks for your unconditional love and uncanny ability to provide comic relief. You are each a precious treasure and we can't wait to see how King Jesus will use you in His kingdom.

Thanks to Cynthia Couch and Saundra Hardesty for reading manuscript drafts and correct-ing my grammar. Thanks to Francis Knox for always opening her home in Jamaica Beach for me to finish writing projects that I can't seem to complete at home. Thanks to the good people at Randall House and the entire D6 family. Ron, Matt, and Michelle, you have been a huge blessing to me personally and a catalyst for a significant move of God! Keep on! Thanks also to my band of brothers: Ryan Rush, Mark Holmen, Jay Strother, Steve Wright, Randy Stinson, Timothy Jones, Richard Ross, Rob Rienow, John Trent, and Kurt Bruner. It is a blessing to serve King Jesus with you in such an exciting way.

CONTENTS

FOREWORD

You are holding in your hand a wonderful parenting plan. I will tell you right from the beginning, this plan works. It's not simple, not always easy, but it works. The plan has at the core of its foundation an ancient text. We call those ancient writings the Bible. The Bible, of course, is the Word of God, and although it was not written as a parenting manual, it contains the truth you need to develop a practical parenting plan giving you the best shot at building a legacy of faith with your family. Unfortunately, too many people parent by circumstance and chance. Some families put more time and energy into planning their annual family vacation than energizing their children's spiritual lives. We know we are to build a legacy of faith from generation to generation but we just don't know what to do. If you read this book, you will be pointed in exactly the right direction.

My wife, Cathy, and I were not raised on the principles of this book. We are first-generation Christians and frankly, when we got married and started raising children, we had no idea what it meant to parent toward a legacy. Like so many others in our generation, we were just trying to make it through Friday. We experimented. We reacted and overreacted. We imitated our own parents and then tried to do just the opposite at other times. There were times we lost heart and grew weary. We have experienced our deepest ecstasy and strongest struggles in the parenting arena. Raising our three daughters to become responsible adults who love God is part joy and part guerrilla warfare! Yet today we would say that our greatest calling in life is to build a legacy of faith from generation to generation.

This book will give you a foundation and plan to develop a common purpose to your parenting. I have the rare privilege on almost a daily basis to interview parenting and family experts through my radio broadcast. I have read hundreds of books on parenting. I absolutely love this book! It's foundational. It's practical. It will help you develop a common language to your parenting and family life. Too often we parent by trial and error without a clear picture of our objectives or end goal. This book will help you find your place in building a legacy.

Brian Haynes is a new and fresh voice in the world of family ministry. He brilliantly challenges us to build our home on the rock of Scripture rather than the moving sands of modern-day culture. His biblical references are right on target. How he and his wife are passionately parenting their own children is nothing short of inspiring. His authenticity oozes from these pages. He can teach us how to have a "heart connection" with our kids because he and Angela are doing just that.

In this book you will learn and then apply these principles and more...

- *Build your parenting upon a foundation.* It's all about priorities, developing a plan and staying focused on what is most important.

- *Be intentional.* Praying for and with your children, celebrating their milestones, and bringing faith conversations into the home are all habits of the heart that come by being proactive.

- *Keep your priorities in order.* We are reminded to put God first as well as be faithful to our commitment to our spouse and not have a child-focused marriage.

Nobody said parenting was going to be easy. Frankly, there are times when really good parents have kids who still rebel. But all authorities tell us that when parents develop an intentional spiritual plan, they have a much better potential of raising children who will love God, love their neighbor, and teach those same truths to the next generation. You have made a great decision to read this book. Blessings on your home.

Jim Burns, PhD
President, HomeWord
Author of *Confident Parenting, Teenology,*
and *The Purity Code*

PREFACE

I walked her to the end of my driveway and watched her shuffle down the street to hang out at a friend's house. As I watched my daughter get farther and farther away and then finally go into the house I contemplated the moment as a picture of our family life with our children. It stirred in me a sense of urgency and longing to love more and lead well in the days that Angela and I have with our children before they launch into life outside of our home. As I walked back up my driveway a tear came to my eye as I longed to live every moment possible with my kids and give them the best gift a parent could give: a deep, life-altering faith in Jesus Christ.

If you are reading this book, you share my sentiment. We all want to make the most of the time we have with our children. As Christian parents, we long to pass on a biblical faith to our children that will trickle into the generations to come. We desire to help our children know the Bible and follow Christ while living in a world that values neither. The question is how?

I am not a parenting expert. Consider me a fellow sojourner who is struggling to be a godly, biblically driven, husband and parent. As a pastor, I have the privilege of working with all types of families and learning from their experiences. Whether they have a brand new baby, four kids and a dog, high school students, or kids that have grown up and left home; broken, blended, single, traditional, whatever… they all have a common need. They need a plan for influencing their children biblically.

The Legacy Path is just that. It is a plan for intentional spiritual parenting. I have been equipping parents to walk this path for years now and I have seen first hand how God meets families that intentionally pursue Him in the every day of life.

The Legacy Path is bigger than just our kids. The journey you are about to take is likely to impact many generations to come. I want my children and my grandchildren and their children to set their hope in God. I am discovering that how we lead our children now matters even to the generations we will never know. That simple truth astounds me. As you discover spiritual parenting consider the words of the Psalmist as he considers biblical legacy.

I will open my mouth in a parable; I will utter dark sayings from old, things that we have heard and known that our fathers have told us. We will not hide them from their children but tell to the coming generation the glorious deeds of the Lord, and his might, and the wonders that he has done. He has established a testimony in Jacob and appointed a law in Israel, which he commanded our fathers to teach their children, that the next generation might know them, the children yet unborn, and arise and tell them to their children, so that they should set their hope in God and not forget the works of God, but keep his commandments. —Psalm 78:2–7

CHAPTER 1

THE THEOLOGY OF LEGACY

I know what you're thinking. You picked up a book on parenting not theology. Sometimes the word "theology" itself intimidates people. It really should not. Theology literally means "the study of God." Why start a parenting book with theology? In a world of relativism it is important for parents to know the unchanging truth of God and His plan to build faith into the next generation. Passing on a legacy of biblical faith to the next generation has always been a part of God's plan.

Permit me to start at the root of our Christian faith. The Scripture teaches that God heard the cry of the Hebrew people, as they were held in bondage to Egypt for 400 years.[1] God loved the Hebrew people as His chosen ones. He often calls them His children.[2] He raised up a Hebrew Egyptian prince turned Bedouin shepherd named Moses to bring His people out of Egypt and into what the Bible calls "the best of all the lands," and "a land flowing with milk and honey." A land with "houses you did not build" and "orchards and vineyards you did not plant." He wanted His children to have the best.[3] It was more than land though. He wanted His children, the people of Israel, to do life His way because it was best for them.

> Passing on a legacy of biblical faith to the next generation has always been a part of God's plan.

God made a covenant with His people much like a marriage. He said, "You will be my people and I will be your God." The Israelite people consummated the marriage by stating they would love God by keeping His instructions. The people told stories of the greatness of God; how He parted the Sea of Reeds and delivered them from the Egyptians, guiding them into a land promised to them as part of the covenant. They remembered His greatness and recognized that He was God and they were not; at least for a little while. Soon they forgot their Deliverer and began chasing gods like Baal and Asherah, sacrificing their own children like the pagans. What happened? How did God's children become a generation of people worshiping the fictitious gods of the pagans?

It only took a few years. One generation of God's people walked off the path of biblical legacy.

As God was helping His people detox from 400 years of Egyptian influence, He demonstrated how they should live as detailed in the first five books of the Bible. He gave clear instructions for how to propagate a culture that would live His way throughout the generations. God's plan for spiritual formation is clearly stated in Deuteronomy 6:4-9.

"Hear, O Israel: The LORD our God the LORD is one. You shall love the LORD your God with all your heart and with all your soul and with all your might. And these words that I command you today shall be on your heart. You shall teach them diligently to your children, and shall talk of them when you sit in your house, and when you walk by the way, and when you lie down, and when you rise. You shall bind them as a sign on your hand, and they shall be as frontlets between your eyes. You shall write them on the doorposts of your house and on your gates."

Deuteronomy 6 is the essence of the legacy path. One generation passing down the faith to the next in the every day of life. The plan is simple. A generation of adults loves God with every fiber of their being and demonstrates what that kind of life looks like by merely living in plain view of the younger generation. Part two of the plan is that a generation of parents intentionally teaches the Words of God diligently to their children in the normal aspects of life, like just sitting at home or walking along the street or going to bed and getting up.[4] It only takes one generation of parents to forsake their role as faith trainers for a culture passionate about God to turn from Him and embrace the gods, the belief systems, and lifestyle of the pagans. Could this be happening in our generation?

What Is The Legacy Path?

According to the dictionary legacy is "anything handed down from the past, as from an ancestor or predecessor."[5] Generally this is true. We are all handing down a certain legacy to our children whether authentically God filled, absolutely hypocritical, or devoid of His truth. Biblical legacy is more than that. Biblical legacy involves molding the heart and soul of the younger generation by passing them faith in the God of our fathers and a life characterized by His presence. A path is, "a way beaten, formed, or trodden by others."[6] The legacy path is an intentional way to lead the next generation to faith in Jesus in the way trodden by others. A path always has a destination. In this case the journey produces a new generation of Christ-followers living according to a biblical worldview and able to pass the faith on to the next generation. The journey produces a generation of children emerging as adults who know how to love God and love people and equip their own sons and daughters to do the same. The legacy path changes the culture, as we know it, moving our children and grandchildren toward life God's way instead of life as is often right in the eyes of the world.

> **The legacy path is an intentional way to lead the next generation to faith in Jesus in the way trodden by others.**

What Is God's Role?

Sometimes I am mortified that I will mess up the whole "daddy" thing. In Christendom we place so much emphasis on being a good parent that we often forget we are utterly dependent on the perfect Father. This should bring an overwhelming sense of shalom to you as a parent. I use the word shalom for a reason. Shalom is often translated into English as "peace." While basically true this is not the whole meaning of shalom. When we rely on God to help us as parents we depend on the author and model of legacy. We cling to a God who knows what to do and how to lead us on the really good days and really bad days. The essence of shalom is a peace and an indescribable contentment that comes from a keen awareness and faith in God who is in control. I find shalom in understanding God's role in the passing of the faith to the next generation, especially when I am a lousy father.

GOD IS THE MASTER PLANNER

We do not make our own path. God is the architect of the brilliant plan to capture the hearts of the generations. God instituted the family. Marriage was His idea (Genesis 2:21-25). Children are His blessing to us just as we are a blessing to Him (Psalm 127:3-5). From the very beginning God designed the family as the vehicle to pass on a heritage of faith, a godly legacy to the next generation. Consider the original promise to Abraham in Genesis. Listen to the language as you read in Genesis 17:4-7:

> *"Behold my covenant is with you, and you shall be the **father** of a multitude of nations. No longer shall your name be called Abram, but your name shall be Abraham, for I have made you the **father** of a multitude of nations. I will make you exceedingly fruitful, and I will make you into nations, and kings shall come from you. And I will establish my covenant between me and you and **your offspring** after you **throughout their generations** for an everlasting covenant to be God to you and to **your offspring after you**."*

In His sovereignty God constructs the foundation of biblical faith on the heart of a righteous man. In the eyes of God, Abraham becomes a father who is a conduit for God's spiritual formation plan for the generations. Without Abraham, you and I would know nothing of Christ. Without Abraham the biblical accounts that comfort and encourage the heart of the Christian would be lost. In a sense… no father, no legacy of faith. God gives Abraham an unbreakable promise and a true story to tell the generations beginning with his own family. It does not end there. God becomes Abraham's Father leading him, providing everything His son needs for the journey. On the legacy path, God does not leave us alone as parents trying desperately to hurl a legacy of faith into the next generation.

> God is the architect of the brilliant plan to capture the hearts of the generations.

SHEPHERD AND GUIDE

Repeatedly in the Scriptures God describes Himself as our shepherd. In a passage on the greatness of God, Isaiah describes the Father this

4

way. *"He will tend his flock like a shepherd; he will gather the lambs in his arms; he will carry them in his bosom, and gently lead those that are with young."*[7] John, a close disciple of Jesus, records the words of the King in John 10:11. *"I am the good shepherd. The good shepherd lays down his life for the sheep."* Gone are the days that this imagery connects with the average Westerner but it is crucial for us as parents to understand.

Shepherds in the Eastern context of the Bible don't shepherd using four-wheelers or horses. They don't drive sheep but instead they lead them. They walk among the flock. A good shepherd leads the sheep to the best places described biblically as green pastures, living water, refuge and shade. The shepherd cares for the sheep knowing each one of them by name. He knows the personalities of his sheep. Perhaps the greatest source of comfort for me as a parent is the understanding that God as the Good Shepherd is a guide who leads me along paths I have never walked before. Let's face it. We have to walk some unfamiliar, even scary paths as parents. He knows the way and He knows the obstacles along the path. He knows me. He knows my wife. He knows my kids. He knows the destination and He knows how to guide us there. As parents we need to follow the Good Shepherd. Clearly part of God's role on the legacy path is to shepherd us and guide us as parents leading our children to embrace life in Christ. Since God developed the plan He knows the path! That makes Him the perfect guide. We (my wife and I) take enormous comfort in knowing we are not alone as we lead our children spiritually. We follow the best Shepherd!

YOUR FATHER

I often forget what it means to be a child. In the serious world of being a husband and father, ministering to people and studying God's Word, what a joy it is to find that I still get to be a kid…and not just any kid. I am one of God's kids. John 1:12-13 says, *"But to all who did receive him, who believed in his name, he gave the right to become **children of God**, who were born, not of blood nor of the will of the flesh nor of the will of man, but of God."* Wrap your mind around this for a second. You and I, if we are repentant followers of Christ, are children of God. We are God's kids. He is our Father. I think this is important for us to embrace even before we attempt to lead our own children in the faith.

What does it mean to have a father in God and to be His child even as we are parents ourselves? Having a father and being His child comes with privilege and responsibility. At its core the Father and child relationship between God and His people can be described in one word: love. A quick study of a familiar passage shows just what kind of love God expends toward His people. You know The Ten Commandments. Consider Exodus 20:5. *"You shall not bow down to them or serve them, for I the* LORD *your God am a jealous God, visiting the iniquity of the fathers on the children to the third and fourth generation of those who* **hate** *me, but showing* **steadfast love** *to thousands of those who* **love** *me and keep my commandments."* The word for hate in this verse is the Hebrew word "sane" meaning to move away from in terms of distance. So the hater of God is not so much the emotive and angry God hater but instead the one who distances himself from the Father. When we love God we "ahav" Him. This is also a term of distance. "Ahav" is loving God in a way that we come closer to Him. When we love Him we take steps toward him by living His way as seen in the latter phrase of the verse. The Father however loves us with a steadfast love. The Hebrew word is "chesod," a completely different word for love than "Ahav". "Chesod" is even more than steadfast love. It's the only way God knows how to love. To quote my friend George DeJong, "He loves you full bore."[8] He never loves at a distance. He always loves us completely, all over us, and in our face. I need the love of the Father to survive the journey and do my part on the legacy path. We have the best Father. Our job is to get our kids to hold hands with Him. I will mess up some days. He never will. He is the Father. He is the One who has loved you every day of your life. He is your Father and He loves you full bore.

BUILDER OF HEART CONNECTIONS

I remember holding Hailey, our firstborn daughter, minutes after she was born. You should know I truly do not cry very easily. As I held her, I looked at the miracle in my arms named Hailey and I wept tears of joy and tears of love. The very same thing happened when Madelyn was born. When Eden came I thought I would be a pro and get through the moment without crying. How is it that I could love someone so much that I had only just met? It is because God built a heart connection between Angela and me and our girls that manifested instantaneously. Angela would tell you and most moms would agree, that she sensed a deep heart connection the moment she realized a new life was growing in her womb. God is a builder of heart connections between parents and their children.

Today I am riding a bus between Petra and Mount Nebo in modern day Jordan. I am huddled in the back corner writing as we travel the land of the Bible. This morning I hiked down the ancient mountain passage way cut by the finger of God leading to Petra, the ancient necropolis made famous by the Indiana Jones Trilogy. I rode a burro up the mountain and had lunch with the Sheik of Petra at his invitation. When I get off the bus I will hike to the top of Mount Nebo and contemplate Moses' thoughts as he looked into the Promised Land he would not enter. Exciting stuff! Yet today, my thoughts are with my fifth grade daughter who is graduating from elementary school. My heart is connected with hers spiritually and emotionally because our God is a builder of heart connections.

PROTECTOR OF THE NAME

God is passionately concerned about His renown and His namesake throughout the generations. *"For my name will be great among the nations says the LORD of Hosts,"* in Malachi 1:11b. Since the beginning of time God has been obsessed with helping each generation know His name. Romans 1:19-20 tells us that God hangs His Name in plain sight for all to see. *"For what can be known about God is plain to them, because God has shown it to them. For his invisible attributes, namely, his eternal power and divine nature, have been clearly perceived, ever since the creation of the world, in the things that have been made. So they are without excuse."* God begins by glorifying His Name in the creation we walk around in every day. Sometimes we are too busy to notice. As if this were not enough, God reveals and glorifies His Name in life altering ways. Consider the words of Jesus as he contemplated his impending death. *"'Now is my soul troubled. And what shall I say? 'Father save me from this hour'? But for this purpose I have come to this hour. Father, glorify your name.' Then a voice came from heaven: 'I have glorified it and I will glorify it again'"* (John 12:27-28). I think often we focus on the fact that Jesus died for the sins of the world. That is certainly part of it.

What we tend to forget is that as much as he loved us and died for our sins, he embraced trial, persecution, and crucifixion to glorify the Name of the Most High God.

God's extreme efforts to make His name famous in each and every life brings us much needed encouragement as the primary faith trainers of our children. Get this. As much as we are concerned about leading our children to walk with Christ, the Creator of the Universe is even more so! The Lord is intimately involved in their lives as their Creator, their Father, and their Good Shepherd. He is passionate about glorifying His Name in their lives. I am so excited He is at work perfectly in my daughters' lives even when I am sleeping. He wants them to know His Name and He wants them to be champions for Christ. We can trust the Father to glorify His Name in the lives of our children.

RADICALLY DEPENDABLE

Malachi 3:6 says, *"For I the LORD do not change."* An old man bound to a wheel chair lived in a brownstone somewhere in the Northeast. Every day the man would wheel himself to his little balcony to watch an ever-changing world hurriedly go by on the street below. An author lived in the unit just below the old man. Each day he would grab a cup of coffee walk outside and look up at the old man. "What's the good news?" he would ask the man watching the world go by. "Middle C," the old man would answer. "Middle C?" the author inquired. "Yes sir, Middle C. The choir may be off a bit on Sunday, you may lose your job tomorrow, and who knows what world event will change the economy in a millisecond. Middle C was Middle C 3000 years ago, it is Middle C today, and it will be Middle C three thousand years from now." In a quickly changing world it is important to know we serve a God, who like Middle C, never changes. He is the same yesterday, today, and forever.

The unchanging nature of God makes Him radically dependable when it comes to fulfilling His role on the legacy path. We can trust Him to do His part. He never changes. This has certain magnificent implications. When you have the worst day of your life as a parent, God does not change. When your child becomes a teenager and morphs before your eyes, God does not change. Whether it is the best of times or the worst of times, God does not change. He is radically dependable. We parent in a world that is always changing. We navigate turbulent waters and lead our children through treacherous wilderness. Take comfort in the fact that God does not change. He will do His part in the life of your children! He always has been and always will be the lead role on the legacy path.

> **Whether it is the best of times or the worst of times, God does not change. He is radically dependable.**

WHAT IS OUR ROLE ON THE LEGACY PATH?

Our God is a big God. The biggest says the Scripture. I think because He is so big that we, as His kids, are expected and empowered to dream big dreams and to pray big prayers. I have an incredibly huge dream. I am dreaming of a new generation of Christ-followers who live to love God passionately and to love people practically in every aspect of life. I am dreaming of a day when the Western culture makes a dramatic change because the leaders of that culture consider the Words of God before they make decisions. I am praying for God to give us a generation. It will only take one to radically change the culture. Can you imagine a day when family is restored in our culture because young adults approach marriage and family biblically? Can you imagine a day when the priorities of the great nations of the world reflect the priorities of God? Believe it or not your role as a parent in this legacy journey is potentially that cataclysmic.

FOLLOW DANGEROUSLY

Christianity is not a passive faith. It requires action on our part. Our culture suggests that Christianity is a religion equal in value to every other religious preference. It is possible to view Christianity, as a box to check off that requires Sunday morning church attendance and not much else. This, however, is not the Christianity of the Bible. When defining what it means to be a Christian, Jesus said, *"If anyone would come after me, let him deny himself and take up his cross daily and follow me."*[9] These words convey a much different lifestyle than the meager Christianity of church on Sunday.

The next generation needs to see their parents following Christ dangerously. It is incredibly uncomfortable and counter-cultural to follow Christ in the everyday of life. Jesus describes it as picking up the same instrument of death used to crucify Him and completely denying yourself. Perhaps this is your most important role in the legacy project: living a holistically Christian life based on a biblical worldview. Our kids need to see what it looks like to follow Christ more than they need to hear what it is like. You and I are the models of following Christ. I would like to say that I find this easy but I do not. I struggle with telling my kids to follow me as I follow Christ because there are days I completely mess it up. It is a struggle to pick up my cross and deny myself daily. This is what it takes to follow Christ and to lead the next generation to do the same. We need to follow dangerously close to the Good Shepherd. Sometimes the King asks us to be so close to Him that we have to exercise great faith, pray horrendous prayers, and endure intense struggle only for the sake of others. Following this way can be dangerous but it is also inspiring. Our kids will believe our faith when they see us struggling to follow dangerously with great faith. Even as Abraham went to a land far off, Noah built an Ark, David threw a rock at a giant, and Jesus endured a cross, we also are called to live with enormous faith. How are you following? How does your life describe Christianity to your children? Questions worth your time as you connect with your role in the journey along the legacy path.

LOVE GOD PASSIONATELY

What does it mean to love the Lord with all your heart, soul, mind, and strength as Jesus stated in Mark 12:29-30? In a world of convenient Christianity we certainly do not naturally embrace an all-consuming form of the faith. In fact our Western version of Christianity has influenced a generation of Christians to live a compartmentalized form of the faith that does not reflect the essence of following Jesus. When we allow Jesus kingship over only certain compartments of our lives we are able to justify a way of life that is appalling to our Lord who gave everything. This is how we can go to church every Sunday and yet refuse to love our neighbor. This is how a person can memorize The Ten Commandments and yet cheat on income tax or commit adultery. In my view compartmentalized Christianity allows the individual to be king or queen and removes Christ from the throne of our lives in a sinful exercise of free will. As followers of Christ we must walk as he walked and live as he lived. Jesus says in John 14:15, *"If you love me, you will keep my commandments."*

In order to love God passionately we must deal with the issue of the supremacy of Christ. The Bible teaches that Jesus has been and always will be part of the Godhead composed of the Father, the Son, and the Holy Spirit. *"He is the image of the invisible God, the firstborn of all creation. For by him all things were created in heaven, and on earth, visible and invisible, whether thrones or dominions or rulers or authorities—**all things were created through him and for him**. And he is before all things, and in him all things hold together. And he is the head of the body, the church. He is the beginning, the firstborn from the dead, that **in everything he might be preeminent**."*[10] Loving God passionately means bowing to Jesus as King and submitting to His graceful preeminence in our lives. It is only when we follow Him as King that we love Him by obeying His commandments. When we see Him as King and live according to the principles of His Kingdom, our children will follow in time. The strongest Christian parents are those who remain explicitly humble and responsive before Jesus the King.

LOVE MY SPOUSE BIBLICALLY

I have often thought the world has it backwards when it comes to family. Have you ever noticed that when people have children they put all of their energy, time, and money into the development of the kids? It's the way of the world. Who doesn't want to give their kids the best, right? On the other hand, if we are going to do this family thing God's way we must prioritize our spouse over our children. Buried in a passage on how to love like Jesus does, we find clear instruction for loving in the context of family. The Scripture addresses husbands and wives first. God does this because the foundation of the family is biblical marriage. Ephesians 5:22-23 says, *"Wives, submit to your own husbands, as to the Lord. For the husband is the head of the wife even as Christ is the head of the church…"* Quickly the Scripture turns to husbands saying, *"Husbands, love your wives, as Christ loved the church and gave himself up for her."*[11] What is it like for a child to watch as his father, not perfectly but consistently, loves his wife sacrificially? What does a child learn as her mother demonstrates a loving submission to a husband who loves with the heart of a servant? This is a unique model of marriage in our culture. It is a model of marriage God's way. When we love our spouses biblically we give our children security, stability, and important insight into how he or she should approach relationships and family in the years to come. There is nothing quite as impactful to the next generation as parents who authentically love each other according to God's design. Biblical marriage is central to legacy.

LOVE MY CHILDREN BIBLICALLY

The legacy path requires parents to love their children biblically. Most parents in the world love their kids. Biblical love is more than a feeling expressed by giving our children opportunities or good gifts. The Ephesians passage describing how to love like Jesus goes on to suggest an interesting aspect of parental love: intentionality. *"Fathers, do not provoke your children to anger, but bring them up in the discipline and instruction of the Lord."* [12]

I have often contemplated this verse in light of my journey as a parent. There are many times I provoke my children to anger. This type of exasperation occurs when I expect my children to think or live a certain way and they do not. Sometimes they feel my disappointment or anger in a way that hurts them but indicts me. You see, they are provoked to anger either because I have not taught them how to live in the particular situation or because they followed my lead and found that I was living hypocritically as they experienced discipline for acting like me. I think this is the way Christian parents exasperate their children.

Instead, to love them biblically, we have to take the time to teach them how to live according to the Scriptures and we have to live authentically in the very things we are teaching. We are to bring them up in the discipline and instruction of the Lord. Ask yourself this question. How are you intentionally bringing up your child in the discipline and instruction of the Lord beyond bringing them to church on Sunday? Most of the trek takes place the other six days of the week.

BECOME THE PRIMARY FAITH INFLUENCER AND GUIDE

No one has been designed as perfectly as you to be the primary faith influencer in the life of your child. It is God's design for parents to influence the faith of their children for a lifetime. We, as parents, have a high calling to lead our children to walk with Christ. This is the most seminal aspect of the legacy path. Remember how the theology of legacy started? *"You shall teach them diligently to your children, and shall talk of them when you sit in your house, and when you walk by the way, and when you lie down, and when you rise."*[13] The pursuit of this process and this aspect of intentional parenting is our focus for the remainder of the book. How can I be the kind of primary faith trainer who teaches my child to embrace an authentic life in Jesus? This is the question of the hour and its answer is the crux of the legacy path. So where do we start?

ENDNOTES

[1]Exodus 2:23–25.

[2]Exodus 4:22–23.

[3]Deuteronomy 8:7–10.

[4]See also Exodus 10:1–2, Exodus 12:26–28, Exodus 13:14–16, Deuteronomy 6:20–25, Deuteronomy 31:12–13, Psalm 78:1–8, Proverbs 22:6, Psalm 145:4, Joel 1:3, Ephesians 6:1–4.

[5]http://dictionary.com.

[6]http://dictionary.com.

[7]Isaiah 40:11.

[8]underthefigtree.org.

[9]Luke 9:23.

[10]Colossians 1:15–18.

[11]Ephesians 5:25.

[12]Ephesians 6:4.

[13]Deuteronomy 6:7.

Thoughts for Discussion with Your Spouse or Small Group

1. What is "The Legacy Path"?

2. Read Deuteronomy 6:4-9. How is this plan for discipleship evident in your family life?

3. What is God's role in "The Legacy Path"? How can you trust He will do His part?

4. What is your role in "The Legacy Path"? What are you doing well and what are you neglecting related to your role?

5. If you are married how would you describe your relationship with your spouse?

6. Read Ephesians 5:22-33. How does your marriage relationship demonstrate this design for biblical marriage?

7. What does it mean to love our children biblically?

CHAPTER 2

LIFE IN CHRIST
CHRISTIAN PARENTS NEED TO ABIDE

First things first. Before we formulate a plan to disciple our kids can we spend some time together working on us . . . just you and me? The big temptation is to get the cart before the horse. I know, cliché, but it fits here. Go back to Deuteronomy 6:5–6 with me for just a moment. *"You shall love the Lord your God with all your heart and with all your soul and with all your might. And these words that I command you today shall be on your heart."* The way I read it, before we can ever teach our children about a relationship with God we have to love Him passionately, having ingested His Words to the point of having them tattooed on our hearts. Here's a question. Do you?

The greatest obstacle parents have to overcome in leading their children spiritually is their own mediocre or morbidly religious relationship with God accompanied by a juvenile understanding of His Word. Harsh words I wish I did not need to write. I only say it because I recognize this truth in my own life sometimes. It's not all our fault. In days gone by, some pastors have offered you and I a version of Christianity that is utterly Western, completely comfortable, and rather unbiblical. Also, many of us have never been truly discipled ourselves adding to our own confusion about the Scripture and how to live it. I know I must sound angry or legalistic at this point. I'm not. I am however concerned, understanding that the next generation is likely to pursue Christ as far as Christianity seems compelling in our generation. For things to change in our culture, we have to revisit how we walk with Christ. Better to expose the truth and deal with it than attempt to move forward without confronting the core issue.

Do a little self-assessment. How is your relationship with Christ? Is it superficial and religious lacking a compelling reason for anyone else to want what you have, including you? Or, is it a relationship with Jesus that directs your steps, influences every decision, is central to every relationship, and sends you on grand adventures? Is yours a relationship with the King that takes every thought captive and seeks to bring glory to His name? Not one stooped in legalism but instead defined by love. Do you go to Him first when times get tough? Is there any sense of risk involved in your life driven by a zealous love for God? Do you care more about self, success, and stuff or are you motivated by a passion for the Kingdom of God? Do other people see your life and want it because of Christ in you or because of what you have accomplished or amassed? Is the extent of your life in Christ what happens on Sunday morning or is church a biblical community, launching you into the rest of the week? When did you last pray for more than 3 minutes? What was the last Scripture you memorized? What did God say to you from His Word today? I pray that you have affirming answers to all of these questions and you are ready to move forward. There is a chance, however, that you and I need to discover what it means to live life in Christ apart from our role as parents. Your relationship with Jesus is the most important element of the legacy path. We are not seeking perfection here, rather authenticity rooted in a real relationship with Christ.

THE LESSON OF THE VINE (JOHN 15:1–11)

If you don't mind, take some time now to find your Bible. Open it up to John 15. Read all of it. These are the very Words of God. Meditate on the passage for a minute before you read on.

In John 15 Jesus teaches an incredible lesson on what a relationship with Him requires. If we want to be people of biblical legacy, before we can bear spiritual fruit we must learn to abide.

The essence of a daily relationship with Christ can be summed up in one word: "abide." It sounds like such a passive word in English. Something like, "just hang out" or "be near" but it really is much more. Jesus uses a picture that any of His original disciples would totally get. It is a picture right out of every day 1st century Hebrew life. Let me help you pull it into our 21st century context. Jesus uses vines to teach His disciples an important lesson. Since most of us are not owners or workers of vineyards we need a little help here. Jesus begins by explaining that He is the "true vine" and the Father is the "vinedresser." He is sharing with us the order of things. He is telling us how things work in His Kingdom. God the Father is caretaker of the entire vineyard. He watches over the vines to make sure they are healthy and producing fruit. He is a loving vinedresser keenly interested in the production of fruit.

Jesus is the "true vine." If I could, I would take you to a vineyard below Tel Lachish where I often stop as I lead groups hiking through Israel to gain an understanding of the biblical narrative. There is a picture there you need to see. Imagine standing in the vineyard looking at hundreds of vines with luscious grapes hanging from them. Follow the branches (which we mistakenly call vines) with your eyes from the grapes down the branches to a small stump growing out of the earth. The stump is the true vine. If properly cared for, the true vine or the root can last an eternity. The true vine is the source of nourishment for the branches that ultimately produce beautiful fruit. Apart from the vine the branches will wither and die. According to the Scripture, Jesus is the true vine providing everything we need as long as we stay connected.

You and I are the branches according to John 15:5. If you go with me in your mind back to the vineyard, focus on the stump or the true vine. Follow the true vine up from the earth to the long branches. The branches stem from the true vine and they grow long and lush in order to produce fruit. Here is the picture. If we, as the branches, stay connected to the true vine (Jesus), we will naturally bear fruit. If we become disconnected from the true vine we will not produce fruit.

WHAT IS FRUIT?

Let's carry the illustration out a bit farther. If you are in a grape vineyard and the true vines are all grape vines then of course the branches will produce grapes. In the same vein if we as Christ-followers are the branches connected to Jesus, the true vine, we will produce fruit in the image of Christ. We will produce other Christ-followers. This is important to understand in light of the legacy path. Part of our fruit production involves our own children. As parents it is imperative we abide in Christ for our own souls but also so our children would become part of the spiritual fruit we produce. Ask yourself a very important question. Does my daily relationship with God nourish my children spiritually? Are my kids growing as "healthy fruit" because of the authenticity of my life in Christ?

Fruit, according to Jesus, is evidence we are his disciples. *"By this my Father is glorified, that you bear much fruit and so prove to be my disciples."* [1] Producing fruit is making disciples. When we reproduce spiritually we glorify the Father and prove we in fact are disciples of Jesus. When we bear fruit we also ensure biblical legacy is cast into the next generation. Please know I am now approaching discipleship from the parent perspective. I do not see the parent-child relationship as the totality of God's plan for discipleship. Jesus did say to His disciples in Matthew 28:18-20, *"All authority in heaven and earth has been give to me. Go therefore and make disciples of all nations, baptizing them in the name of the Father and of the Son and of the Holy Spirit, teaching them to observe all that I have commanded you."* This Great Commission certainly is not just for parents rather it is for every Christ-follower. However, when an adult Christ-follower has children, it is then his or her responsibility to disciple them in the context of family.

For a very long time parents have depended on children's pastors or youth pastors to disciple their kids. This is a great partnership but it does not take the place of parent to child faith training. You and I as parents realize primarily God has entrusted our children to our care and we are to infuse their lives with Christ as we abide in Him. We are not the only people God will use to form our children spiritually but we are the primary faith trainers. Discipleship is not merely the work of your church's ministry team. They can help but we as parents are the 24/7 branches, abiding in Christ so our children might become disciples who eventually produce their own fruit as they abide in Christ. This is how faith in the Most High God bears the fruit of legacy from generation to generation.

> For a very long time parents have depended on children's pastors or youth pastors to disciple their kids. This is a great partnership but it does not take the place of parent to child faith training.

HOW CAN I ABIDE IN CHRIST?

To abide in Christ requires considerable effort. The effort is typically a joy, but it is a disciplined work nonetheless. I find it much easier to drift away from Christ, becoming disconnected and practically useless. So what do you and I need to do in order to abide? A cursory study of the gospels reveals at least seven key disciplines Jesus teaches His disciples to practice. I believe each of these disciplines is central to abiding and are particularly characteristic of an authentic life in Christ. For our purpose now, let's focus on only two of these disciplines for abiding in Christ. I consider this the "1-2 punch" when it comes to the basics of abiding. In a way these are "no brainers." These disciplines become life transforming when approached in a fresh way. Struggle with these core competencies of life in Christ, not as a religious person seeking to check off more "I'm a good Christian" boxes but instead as a lover of Christ keenly interested in abiding in Him, producing fruit as natural evidence of your connectedness with Him. View these disciplines as a new way of living. Our opportunity to abide is a picture of grace in and of itself. Jesus wants you to stay connected to Him. He wants to nourish you and use you in exciting ways for His namesake. You and I get to abide!

1. PRAYER

Prayer is communication with God. It is an amazing experience where we get to quiet ourselves before the King of the Universe, pour out our hearts and listen to what He might have for us. Prayer is essential to abiding in Christ. On several occasions Jesus' disciples begged Him to teach them how to pray His way. His young followers asked Him how to pray because they were moved by His intimacy with the Father and they realized His connection with God in prayer was a clear source of power and authority. They were also disciples following their Rabbi so naturally they wanted to learn to pray just like He prayed.

Jesus teaches His disciples how to pray in Matthew 6:5–18. Take a moment to read it.

This is the section of Scripture from which Christendom derives "the Lord's Prayer." As Jesus is teaching, He pleads with His disciples not to be like the "hypocrites" who pray so everyone can see their religiosity.[2] The word "hypocrite" is a theatrical term used for "actor." Prayer is not for everyone else to see so they can judge your faith. Prayer is intimate communication between you and the Father made possible through Jesus. Prayer is not an act but instead a real and ongoing conversation between you and God. Jesus says when we pray we should go into our room and shut the door to be alone with God.

This is way beyond the obligatory prayer offered at mealtimes and bedtimes. This process of prayer is offered in pursuit of intimacy. It is crucial for abiding. Do you have a daily prayer time that looks anything like that?

I go through seasons where I am utterly committed to prayer alone with the Father. Other times I let the encroachments of life intrude on my prayer time. Sometimes the urgency of email, a phone call, a family situation or a person in need of care becomes my focus leaving my time of prayer until the next day. Soon several days of urgency lead to a season of prayerlessness. In my life there is a direct correlation to my connectedness with the Father and my daily commitment to prayer. If I pray I abide. If I don't, I won't. I would be willing to say that the same is true for you.

Here are some practical suggestions for abiding through prayer. Schedule your time alone. Give it a permanent spot in your daily schedule and protect the time. This can be practically difficult but it is worth the fight. This is also not an absolute. I think particularly of busy moms. Maybe you have little ones at home who wake up early and go hard all day. Maybe you choose to pray during afternoon naps and the time on that varies a little from day to day. Perfect. It is your commitment to pray when the house gets quite that counts. Don't feel defeated because you can't schedule it and pray exactly on time every day. If you do you will soon quit praying and that would be a travesty.

Prayer is as important as breathing when it comes to an abiding life in Christ.

If you can pray in the morning you will find wisdom and peace for the rest of the day's demands. I will often bring my daily calendar and pray over the decisions, meetings with people, and family moments I will have that day. It is an amazing experience to pray the Words of God. I like to pray the Psalms as they are often written as prayers. Certainly Jesus provides the best prayer pattern in Matthew 6:9–13. Often people repeat the model prayer as a regurgitation of words memorized. We say it as fast as we can without considering the implication of each phrase. This is exactly what Jesus was talking about when He said, *"And when you pray, do not heap up empty phrases as the Gentiles do, for they think that they will be heard for their many words."* [3] Instead view the prayer as a pattern designed to help us know how to pray.

Pray a phrase and then meditate on it. For instance pray, *"Our Father in heaven, hallowed be your name."* [4] This is an opportunity to worship. Tell God how holy He is. Search the Scriptures for the different names used to describe God and pray them giving thanks that our God is the Holy God of the Universe. Pray, *"Your kingdom come, your will be done, on earth as it is in heaven."* [5] This is an act of submission. You are realigning your life with the fact that God's will supersedes yours in every area of life. This is a great time to pray for your family. I will often say, Lord, will your kingdom come and your will be done in Angie's life (and Hailey's, Madelyn's, and Eden's) focusing on specific areas of intercession for my wife and our three daughters. Before I know it, I am only halfway through the model prayer and thirty minutes have gone by. Do the same thing for each phrase of Jesus' prayer and you will easily pray for an hour. You will also find you are abiding in ways you never imagined. Prayer is as important as breathing when it comes to an abiding life in Christ.

Don't forget to pray big prayers. You and I serve a God that is exponentially huge. His greatness is impossible to get your mind around. I have no problem praying magnificent prayers since our God is so capable. In the same passage on abiding, Jesus says in John 15:7 *"If you abide in me, and my words abide in you, ask whatever you wish, and it will be done for you."* The beauty of abiding in Christ and the Scripture is that we will typically pray the heart of God. He answers when we align with His will. When we pray big prayers aligned with His will we find unimaginable answers.

In my Bible next to John 15 I have several prayer requests written down that I ask for consistently believing John 15:7. Here are a few of them:

• Lord, let our girls become dangerous "fruit bearers" in Your kingdom for Your namesake.

• Lord, bless my wife in unimaginable ways by allowing her to watch

Your legacy through her play out in the lives of our daughters and future grandchildren over time.

- Father, give me a platform from which to preach the Word to the world.

- Father, give me an entire generation of American's who will abide in You and lead their children to do the same thus drastically changing our culture.

- Lord, give me influence with pastors and ministry leaders all around the world to help them see the importance of strategic partnerships between church and home.

- Lord give me a community of believers, a church willing to do what it will take to influence the world for Christ and will live out the Great Commission beginning in their own homes.

Selfish prayers? I don't think so because they are completely in line with the heart of God and stem from an understanding of Scripture. Big prayers? Yes, but God is so much bigger. How He chooses to answer those prayers is up to Him. I, on the other hand, must continue to abide in faith and pray big. Make your own list of biblically based "big prayers." You will be amazed how God chooses to further His legacy through your life and your family!

2. SCRIPTURE

Why is it that Jesus says, *"If you abide in me, and **my words abide in you,** ask whatever you wish, and it will be done for you?"* [6] Why does Jesus say, *"If anyone loves me, he will **keep my word.**"* [7] Why does God the Father say in a portion of the Shema found in Deuteronomy 6:6, *"And these **words that I command you today shall be on your heart"**?* Perhaps it is because knowing and practicing the Word of God is essential to living life in relationship with Him. There is something about loving God that involves ingesting His Word consistently. So here is the million-dollar question. Do the Words of Christ abide in you?

It is not as if we can't understand the Scriptures. We know we should be reading God's Word and we even feel guilty when we neglect time in the Bible. Too many of us view the Bible as difficult, lofty, or even irrelevant. We feel defeated because we are not even sure where to start reading. I see this as one of Satan's greatest attacks on Christianity. If he can keep you from God's Word, he knows he can keep you from abiding and that renders you spiritually impotent, bringing a screeching halt to legacy in and through your life.

Abiding through reading, studying, and meditating on God's Word is a spiritual discipline. To be honest, I have a difficult time separating prayer and Scripture in practice. When I pray I am in the Scripture and when I am in the Scripture I pray. I would like to say my study of the Text is consistent and exhilarating all of the time. In reality, I struggle with consistency. There are weeks I literally crave the Word eagerly waiting for my time alone with God. There are other times I have to make myself sit down to read just a very few words. Sometimes I read the Word and wonder what in the world God is trying to say to me. Other times it is as if God leans in and speaks to me through a giant megaphone while standing only inches away from my face. It is His choice to speak but mine to abide.

Everyone has his own unique methods for reading and meditating on the Scriptures. There is not one right way or wrong way. If you are new to this and would like a suggestion or two on how to start studying the Bible, let me offer a couple of thoughts I find practical.

- First, set aside a time and a place. You and I are more likely to read the Scriptures consistently if we have a scheduled time and place to make it happen.

- Choose a solid translation you can read and understand.

- If you like to write, keep a journal and write down the things God brings to mind as you read the Bible.

- Bible reading plans are good, but I often feel like they ask me to read so much in a day that I can't adequately think about what God is saying through the Word.

My quirky pattern goes like this. I read a chapter in Proverbs every day. There are 31 chapters so you just flip to the chapter that corresponds with the calendar date and read. I have been doing this for about twenty years and I am still learning new things from God through His words in the book of Proverbs.

I am also always reading another book of the Bible. Right now I am reading the book of Daniel. I like to alternate between the Old Testament and the New Testament. So, when I finish Daniel I will pick a New Testament book. I read a chapter, meditate on it, pray through it, listen to God, write down anything that pops, and go on about my day. For me this is abiding by staying in the Scriptures. People who abide in Christ spend time in the Scriptures.

The Scripture is important for your everyday life. If we are Christ-followers then by definition we are actively "following" him. How will you know where Jesus is going so you can follow if you do not know His words? How will you know what to do or how to make decisions if you can't hear God by listening to His Word? As Christ-followers we are God's chosen people. He wants to lead us, converse with us, and give us peace in our hearts. Colossians 3:16-17 says, *"Let the word of Christ dwell in you richly, teaching and admonishing one another in all wisdom, singing psalms and hymns and spiritual songs, with thankfulness in your hearts to God. And whatever you do, in word or deed, do everything in the name of the Lord Jesus, giving thanks to God the Father through him."*

Abiding in Scripture brings wisdom, thankfulness, and peace. Abiding in the Word influences "whatever we do" so we can do it in the name of Christ. This is crucial for legacy. The "whatever we do" in life will be our model to the next generation. It would be best if that model were shaped by the very Words of God.

> The Scripture is important for your everyday life. How will you know where Jesus is going so you can follow if you do not know His words?

Now back to why you originally picked up this book. You are concerned about your kids and how your parenting affects them. My wife and I constantly wonder if we are messing up our kids or leaving a God-honoring legacy. We are realizing more and more we need wisdom that goes beyond our own capacities—wisdom from the God who created our kids and knows the unique design of their minds, hearts, and bodies. We need the Words of Scripture as the foundation of truth in our family. We need to know how to follow God so our kids can follow us as we follow Christ.

Parenting that stems from abiding in the Word of God yields

wisdom, compassion, joy, truth, and peace as invaluable tools necessary for teaching our kids to walk with Christ. 2 Timothy 3:16 and 17 says, *"All Scripture is breathed out by God and profitable for teaching, for reproof, for correction, and for training in righteousness, that the man of God may be competent, equipped for every good work"...**especially parenting Christ-followers** [emphasis mine]. You and I need the Word! Our children need us to abide in the very Words of God.

WHAT JESUS THINKS OF YOU (JOHN 15:14–16)

This has been a challenging and convicting chapter to write. In some ways I have felt as if I have been required to expose some inadequacies in the general nature of western Christianity with a proverbial two by four. If you find yourself convicted understand conviction is a good thing. Conviction is the work of the Holy Spirit to draw you back into an abiding relationship with the true vine, Jesus Christ. Conviction is evidence of God's grace and love for us. Be encouraged by the Words of Christ. Just knowing what He thinks of us is evidenced by His own words at the end of John 15.

"You are my friends if you do what I command you. No longer do I call you servants, for the servant does not know what his master is doing; but I have called you friends, for all that I have heard from my Father I have made known to you. You did not choose me, but I chose you that you and appointed you that you should go and bear fruit and that your fruit should abide, so that whatever you ask the Father in my name, he may give it to you."

—Jesus in John 15:14–16

ENDNOTES

[1]John 15:8.
[2]Matthew 6:5.
[3]Matthew 6:7.
[4]Matthew 6:9.
[5]Matthew 6:10.
[6]John 15:7.
[7]John 14:23.

THOUGHTS FOR DISCUSSION WITH YOUR SPOUSE OR SMALL GROUP

1. Describe the status quo pertaining to your relationship with Jesus Christ. How do you currently "abide" in Christ?

2. What does prayer look like in your life? What needs to change based on your understanding of John 15?

3. What role does Scripture play in your life? How do you know you understand the biblical text and practically apply it?

4. What steps do you need to take to engage in an abiding relationship with God?

5. How could a deeper, abiding relationship with Jesus impact your children and enhance your family legacy journey?

CHAPTER 3

BUILD YOUR HOUSE ON THE ROCK

When I was a teenager we moved from the hills of middle Tennessee to Houston, Texas. Quite a transition if you ask me. We went from the beautiful, hilly suburbs of Nashville to the extreme flat and morbidly humid suburbs of Houston. I will never forget the first summer we were there and experienced a torrential downpour that blew in off the Gulf of Mexico. We got about five inches of rain in an hour and quickly learned that our tiny backyard did not drain properly. In fact, the water rose and came dangerously close to the back door. My mom opened the door and started sweeping water away from the door and out the back gate as fast as she could. The water rushed down the driveway to the street, which was also flooded. My mother was soaked as she fought the water with her yellow broom. She looked at me as we struggled to redirect the water and said, "The wise man built his house on the rock." A little "remez"[1] of her own. What she left out was, "but the foolish man built his house on the sand" and in the path of the flood. I remember thinking, "Mom hates Houston and she believes God thinks we are stupid for living on the sandy, swampy shore of the Gulf of Mexico." For the record, now I like Houston.

It is interesting the Scripture often speaks to the building of "the house." Many times when the Bible refers to "the house" or "the house of" it is referring to a specific family or lineage. One familiar example is found in at the end of Joshua 24:15. *"But as for me and my house, we will serve the LORD."* In a pivotal passage of Scripture, Joshua challenges the people to put away the gods they served beyond the Jordan River and in Egypt and wholly serve the Lord. With the challenge he makes a bold statement relating to his house. Not a dwelling place of stone but "house" as in the people that spring from his own lineage. The house is the people he is responsible for as it pertains to their relationship with God. Interesting thought. Biblically, my house is not the brick façade structure I live in but the generations that flow from me. My house is my family and I am indeed responsible to lead them to serve the Lord not unlike Joshua.

Though I am responsible to lead, it is not my sole responsibility to build the house. God is the architect and builder. If I trust in Him, then He becomes the builder of my house. If I try to build my house by myself, it will likely crumble under the pressure of culture and dysfunction. Psalm 127:1a says, *"Unless the Lord builds the house, those who build it labor in vain."* [2] Is the Lord building your house with your help or are you going it alone?

Jesus told a story once that my mom referenced on that rainy day in Houston. Found in Matthew 7:24–27, Jesus teaches that everyone who listens to His words and does them is like a wise man that built His house on the rock. When the rain fell, the wind blew, and the floods came the house stood strong because it was built on the foundation of the rock. However, people who hear His words and choose not to practice them are like a foolish man who built his house on the sand. The rain fell, and the winds blew, and the flood came and beat against the house *"and it fell, and great was the fall of it."* [3] Lord, in your mercy, keep my house from falling in the storm.

You may know Jesus was a teacher who used what people understood to communicate His message clearly. In Israel where Jesus is teaching the parable, there is only one way to understand this contrasting picture between rock and sand because there is only one place to find sand. You find sand in the bottom of a "wadi." The term "wadi" is a Hebrew word for valley. It is not the lush green valley you might imagine. Rather it is a deep crack cut by the finger of God running between the rocks that form hills and mountains dominating the Israeli terrain from the Dead Sea to the Galilee. When it rains, water in the form of a crushing wall, comes crashing down through the wadi draining from higher elevations. The flood literally destroys everything in its path with unimaginable force. I have seen mangled cars in the wadi that were caught in the floods. I have seen boulders larger than my house literally moved by the force of the wadi washouts. Jesus compares a person who does not practice His way of living to someone who is foolish enough to build his house in the bottom of a wadi. It's only a matter of time until that house will be destroyed. On the other hand, a person who does practice the very Words of Christ is like one who built his house on the rock avoiding the destructive floods of life. Sometimes when we try to build the house our way we build it right in the bottom of the wadi and in the path of a cataclysmic wall of water.

A HOUSE IN THE WADI

How would you know if you are building your house like a foolish man, in vain, and in the path of destruction? People who build their families in the sand view life differently than those who build their houses on the rock. Let's take a look at what a house built in the sand looks like in our day and in our culture.

A house built on the sand embraces a worldview that defines basic life success very differently than Jesus describes. You can tell if you are building your house in the sand by asking yourself this two part question, "What is my view of success and how am I living my life to achieve it?"

Success is an interesting concept developed out of a person's worldview. A foundational issue to settle before defining success is the issue of who God is. Your concept of God will greatly influence your definition of success. Our understanding of God is not the only factor forming our concept of success but it is certainly a driving factor.

For instance, if a person believes God exists for his benefit alone then he truly can define success however he wants and ask God's blessing on it. Sometimes an Americanized version of Christianity fuels this fire. Statements like, "God is on your side" and "God wants you to have your best life right now" turn into foundation stones supporting a view that God exists for you as a sort of genie in the bottle. People, who embrace this Christian form of humanism, if there is such a thing, typically find success doing what is right in their own eyes. This God concept will define success in a way that leads to building your family in the path of the flood. Unfortunately many American Christians embrace this view to a degree.

In Western cultures, Christians who lean toward a God who exists for them define success in terms of health and wealth. As such, success is a healthy life and enough money, at least, to be comfortable. The pursuit of this success can be as maddening as building your house in the sand and counterproductive to the will of God for your "house."

This lifestyle is driven by consumerism and materialism. Important decisions such as, where to live, where to attend school, career choice, who to marry, how many kids to have, and a host of other life choices are sifted through the filter of worldly success. What will happen financially if I make this move, marry this person, have another child, or take a different job in a different location? The outcome of our decision-making in this mode must yield monetary and material results. We even pray that God would find favor (meaning monetarily) on us as we seek to make the best decisions . . . for us. The problem is we are praying for success based on our definition. Not necessarily God's definition. This places us in the driver's seat where we are most comfortable, and allows God to take His place in the genie bottle.

Anything less than that kind of security or success is somehow failure. As long as everyone in the family has good health and the money continues to pour in, God is good. As soon as the rain of life begins, the question from the bottom of the wadi becomes, "Where is God?" because God should ensure "success" meaning prosperity. This is typical of a house built in the sand, or one built in vain by our own hands.

I need to offer a clarifying statement. It is possible to have health and wealth and be like the wise man that built his house on the rock. Money and material possessions were evident in the lives of Bible heroes like Abraham, Joseph, and David. Money is not the issue. Truly, our God concept and definition of success determines whether our house will be built on the rock or in the sand.

In reality, this view of God, life, and success is fairly normative in Western Christianity. I know because I struggle with it as the leader of my own home. A life centered in this kind of success is often very busy. It has to be. After all, as parents in this worldview, we want our kids to have the best opportunities for success so they too can have health and wealth. So at a very early age we involve them in a host of extracurricular activities on top of making sure they attend an exemplary school. We get them involved in as many things as possible to give them as much chance as possible for personal success. Add to that our own careers often pursued by both adults in the family for the sake of personal fulfillment, chasing a healthier and wealthier lifestyle. What you have left is a life with no margin left to be intentional about passing biblical legacy from parent to child.

Though all of these activities are good things, they absorb time and money taking away our opportunities as parents to offer them the best eternal things. Does this sound like your life? There are days my life looks just like this. There is a different way.

A HOUSE ON THE ROCK

On the other hand if your understanding of God is that you exist for Him, then He defines success for your life and you willingly align your life with that definition. This understanding of God recognizes His sovereignty as King of the Universe and His love for us that allows us to choose His way of success or our own. People who view the God of the Bible in this way typically find success doing what is right in the eyes of the Lord, intentionally allowing Him to build their house on the rock. This is a completely different way of living.

In this worldview, success is defined in the Scriptures. This is the basic difference. Forming a way of looking at the world and living life based on the very Word of God is the essence of Jesus' teaching of the wise man and the foolish man. The wise man builds his house on the rock, which in the context of the parable is hearing the Scriptures and putting them into practice. If you want your house, your family, to be built on the rock your view of success in life has to be adjusted to fit God's view of success.

One day Jesus was asked which of God's commandments are most important. Jesus said, *"Hear, O Israel: The Lord our God, the Lord is one. And you shall love the Lord your God with all your heart and with all your soul and with all your mind and with all your strength. The second is this: You shall love you neighbor as yourself. There is no other commandment greater than these."*[4]

> **If you want your house, your family, to be built on the rock your view of success in life has to be adjusted to fit God's view of success.**

Clearly Jesus restates the passage called "Shema" from which we started in Deuteronomy 6:4–9 emphasizing the importance of loving the one true God with every fiber of our being. He adds Leviticus 19:18, telling us we should live out our love for God by loving other people. In the view of many Christ-following scholars, this way of living is Jesus' view of success for Christ-followers.[5]

So, if my house is being built on the rock, then my view of God is that I exist for Him. His view of success for my house is to love God wholly by following Christ and by loving other people as Jesus does. For me to be successful as a man in this paradigm I need to love God and love people. To know if I am a success as a husband, I need to ask if I am leading my wife to love God and love people more or if I am an obstacle for her in that way. If we want to know if we are successful as parents we have to ascertain the developing ability of our children to love God with all of their heart, mind, soul, and strength and love their neighbors as themselves.

The legacy path is literally the passing of this view of success from parent to child from one generation to the next. In my view this is the battle we fight for the next generation. The culture is full of people building houses in the sand telling our children to embrace God as a god who exists for them and wants them to have everything. As parents, we have to lead them to realize that "stuff" does not equal success. Transferrable love of God and for people equals success. That is the end goal of the legacy path and the heart of spiritual formation.

People who allow the Lord to build their house on the rock understand that it takes time and intentionality to equip the next generation to love God and love people. Parents seeking to raise children biblically understand that many good things in life compete for our time and intentionality. There is an art to sacrificing the good things to experience the best things. The legacy path requires a lifestyle that values simplicity and time.

1. SIMPLICITY

Simplicity is freedom. Complexity clutters life with chaotic schedules, material possessions to manage and maintain, and unnecessary financial responsibility. Complexity of life, even when filled with good things, monopolizes valuable time and energy necessary to disciple our children, following the model of Deuteronomy 6:7. *"You shall teach them diligently to your children, and shall talk of them when you sit in your house, and when you walk by the way, and when you lie down, and when you rise."* An important question to ask: "Is my life so complex that I don't have time with my children to hang out at home and to go for a walk together or be there when we go to bed and when we get up?" Simplicity buys us time with our children that enables us to disciple them and pass on a godly legacy.

Before we jump into the practical issues of simplicity, I want you to know something about my family. We are a pretty typical, suburban family. Our kids go to school, play sports, and are really involved at church. We have three daughters, which is really great most of the time. Other times I feel really misunderstood as the only man in the house. We have a turtle but I think it's a girl too. My wife is a graduate of Texas A&M. She majored in accounting and was at the top of her class. In the early years of our marriage she worked for a top accounting firm in Dallas and climbed the ladder quickly. Today we live in a booming suburb of Houston. If you ever visit our community you will quickly conclude we typically define success here in terms of position, money, and material possessions. Unfortunately we also add the success of our kids in that mix. You see a lot of "My Child is an Honor Student at…" bumper stickers on minivans and SUV's. I am a pastor in a pretty great suburban church, which is a large responsibility. I write and speak other places adding a whole new dynamic to life balance.

Life for us can be as busy and complex as it is for any family in our particular culture and that my friends, is very busy. Trust me. We know what it means to fight for simplicity in a complex world. I realize every family is not "just like mine." Families are more like snowflakes. Unique in ways I might not even be able to imagine. Therefore the decisions you make about simplifying life might look drastically different than mine. Please do not

> **Complexity of life, even when filled with good things, monopolizes valuable time and energy necessary to disciple our children, following the model of Deuteronomy 6:7.**

read the rest of this chapter as judgmental. I am simply rehashing the issues I have seen countless families deal with as they pursue legacy.

We believe the fight for simplicity creates an environment in our home conducive for faith training and vital to the legacy path. Simplicity equals time and time is what it takes to lead children spiritually. Simplicity is a counter cultural idea in most Western households. Simplicity for the sake of spiritual formation is an even crazier idea to most people. Here are some of the issues you will likely grapple as you think of simplifying your life in order to make life conducive for faith training.

SHOULD SOMEONE STAY HOME?

How important is it for one parent to be at home for the sake of children? Should anyone have to sacrifice career and walk the "stay at home" path or some version of it? Should it be Mom like the traditional conservative viewpoint suggests? I realize this is a very touchy subject in our generation. I once posted a blog[6] on this particular issue and I got positive comments, negative comments, hugs in the hallway at church, and dirty looks by the coffee pot in our workroom at church. It's just one of those issues. Many arguments exist about what is best stemming from the thought arenas of psychology, religion, secular and Christian parenting, and even the blogosphere. The question is what is right? I approach this issue from the perspective of seeking what is best for our families in an attempt to discern God's heart on the matter.

Let's take an honest look at Scripture. The Bible suggests women are in a role by design to "help" as the word is used in Genesis 2:20. The word "helper" used to describe "woman" is largely misunderstood in modern Christendom. The Hebrew root for the world "helper" is *azar*. The word *azar* means more than we grant it in the English language. Some read "helper" in the English and think of the word as subservient and secondary. Reading helper that way allows us to build a dogmatic, conservative, yet tainted worldview that says women must stay home with the children according to the roles of men and women defined by God at creation because she is the 'helper."

The word *azar* does translate helper but it implies much more in the original language. *Azar* means ally, further, help, protect, and support. One picture associated with the word *azar* is that of military assistance.

Azar describes one who comes alongside another in battle. The word *azar* is used to describe the Lord Himself as shown in Exodus 18:4, Deuteronomy 33:29, Psalm 10:14, and Psalm 27:9. In Psalm 118:7 David says, "*The LORD is on my side as my helper.*" I believe we misrepresent the heart of God when we see a woman's role as subservient to the man based on the Creation passage in Genesis 2.

Instead, a better understanding of women is *azar*, which is an equal creation of God who comes alongside, shoulder to shoulder, as an ally to help, protect, and support and to further. This understanding does not change the role of men as leaders but it does broaden the typical understanding of the biblical role of women. This in fact is foundational to our discussion. Should someone stay at home with the kids? Should it be Mom?

Several passages build on our foundational understanding of the role of women in the family. Proverbs 31 describes an excellent wife and mother as one who "*makes linen garments and sells them*"[7] and "*looks well to the ways of her household.*"[8] That biblical picture is one of a woman who works outside the home and stays at home. Certainly, a different cultural context implies that her children may have been involved with her in the work of the business and actually gone with her in the "selling." However, she is working and managing the household. Probably these are not compartmentalized issues in her culture. Today we compartmentalize everything.

Titus 2:5 speaks to the issue from a 1st century context. As a stand alone, outside of the whole counsel of Scripture, this is a hot button passage. Paul says women should, "*be self-controlled, pure, working at home, kind, and submissive to their husbands, that the word of God may not be reviled.*" Clearly Paul's advice for women is to work in the home as followers of Christ. So what is the right answer?

You have the Scripture and as a Christfollower, you have the Holy Spirit who serves as a counselor and a guide to you. I think each family must wrestle with the Scripture, the roles of men and women, and seek the direction of the Holy Spirit. He will provide you with a deep sense of calling and conviction about the issue. Each family may look a bit different. Some may choose for Mom to stay home all the time or for a season. Others may choose to work outside of the home and still manage their family. While difficult, it is not out of bounds biblically.

If we are pursuing life balance and simplicity, I believe it is practically beneficial for Mom to be home at least for a season. After studying the Scripture and praying we chose for Angela to stay home when our first daughter was born. Not without sacrifice especially on Angela's part, this has become the secret to balance in our family. We keep life simple by living on one salary and allowing Mom to focus on the household. This means our children have a parent available to invest in them during work hours. This means we also have a parent who understands our family priorities and works to keep life balance so that we can take steps in the right direction. For us, this was absolutely the right decision. What about you?

SHOULD WE DOWNSIZE?

A common struggle among families who are fighting for simplicity is the issue of downsizing. Certainly not everyone is in this boat. This section is for those who have pursued the American definition of success, found it, and now feel like it is an obstacle to their ability to lead their family spiritually. Sometimes material success snowballs requiring more time and energy than it is worth. If you are asking yourself the question, "How will I ever have the time or energy to train my children spiritually" you might be overcommitted. Sometimes buying time means selling stuff. For instance, if you lived in a smaller house would it free one parent to move from full-time to part-time status or even to stay at home? If you drove different cars would you lower payments or remove payments and buy some precious time together? Building your house on the rock might mean adjusting your lifestyle in pursuit of balance and simplicity. Too much stuff could mean that you are too busy to live life with your children in a way that deepens them as Christ-followers.

2. TIME

Our children need us to spend time with them. Perhaps the first step toward becoming a legacy parent is making a clear commitment to spend time with our children. Many parents think that they are spending time with their children when really they are not. If both parents work it is likely that whoever becomes the chosen day care provider is having more of an impact on our children than are we. When our children start school they spend eight hours a day under the influence of teachers who have a formal platform for influence in their lives. If we view quality time with them as sitting on the sidelines of an athletic event or in the audience of a recital or performance then we have become spectators. It is significant to be there but the real influencer is the coach or instructor. Understand, our children need other influencers in their lives and coaches or instructors are good. However if the bulk of our time spent with our children is sitting on the sidelines while someone else coaches, teaches, or instructs, we are missing our opportunity.

Many suggest quantity time is not necessary but instead it is quality time that is more important. In reality, children need both quantity time and quality time. As I seek to understand God's plan for the spiritual formation of the next generation I find it biblically evident that family play a primary role. If this is true, then as parents, we have to be with our children a lot and we have to have experiences with them that matter. This is both quantity and quality. Quantity speaks to spending time with our kids in the normal moments of life. Check out Deuteronomy 6:7 again. I think sitting in the house, getting up, going to bed, and walking along the road seem like really normal moments in every day life. Are we around for the normal time? Quality time is the phrase we use to describe exciting or important experiences together. Quality time is biblically important as well but if all you have is a little quality time and no quantity time it will be difficult to lead your children spiritually.

FAMILY SCHEDULE

If you have children you know life can get busy really quickly. Pretty soon you are so busy doing all of the good things that you really have no time for what is absolutely best. Even if one parent is home and you have downsized to make more time, a crazy family schedule can be a giant obstacle to living Deuteronomy 6 lives with our children. Consider your family schedule. Are you so busy taking your children to participate in really good things that you have nothing left for

> If the bulk of our time spent with our children is sitting on the sidelines while someone else coaches, teaches, or instructs, we are missing our opportunity.

quality together time? I know what that is like. Here are some helpful boundaries that may alleviate the chaos in your family schedule and restore much needed time together.

- *One Extracurricular Activity per Kid:* We have three children. If each child participates in one event outside of church and school our schedule is more than full. We have set a very clear boundary with each of our children that works effectively. One kid can play one sport or participate in one music class or one art class, but only one per semester. We help them choose based on their natural bent but we limit it to one. Any more than that would steal critical time together. Where I live, this is not the norm. You may have to push back against the norm to maintain time for building legacy.

- *Prioritize Family Time Together:* There should be one night every week reserved for family. For us, Sunday afternoon and evening is perfect, especially because our church shuts down on Sunday night just to give families time together. Sunday becomes like a Sabbath for us. We worship, we eat, we play, and we use the time for intentional "Faith Talks." More on that later. Pick a night and make it yours. Have everyone in the family put it on the schedule and enjoy the time.

- *Maintain Family Dinner Time:* Family dinnertime can be a great time to regroup and discuss the day while simply being together. This is a lost art in busy, success driven, Western cultures. Travel to the Eastern context of the Bible and you will experience the beauty and joy of the family meal. Certainly with a measure of grace and flexibility, families can sit down and eat dinner together most nights of the week. It will not happen without intentionality. Plan for dinner at home and work to get everyone around the table most nights of the week. The family table is a safe place to communicate. Dinner provides a natural time of discussion allowing parents to speak into the lives of their children concerning the events of the day. You may read this, assess your family life, and exclaim, "Impossible!" The legacy pathway will require you to adjust your schedule, creating invaluable time together.

NOW YOU ARE READY

In these first three chapters I monopolized a considerable amount of your time helping you get your house in order as you prepare for the legacy journey. You understand the theology of legacy. You get that your personal relationship with Christ is actually the conduit for biblical faith to transfer to the next generation. You are working on abiding in Christ. You have assessed your situation and determined if you are building your house on the rock or in the sand. You have asked yourself what part God is playing in building your family. You have graciously allowed me to meddle with the very pattern of your life both as a person and as a family unit. These issues are fundamental and provide stability for the path. Now you are ready for a plan. It's time to plan your journey and develop your family strategy for passing an authentic relationship with Christ to the next generation. Join me on the path of legacy milestones.

ENDNOTES

[1]Remez is a rabbinic teaching technique used among people who know the biblical text. It is the art of teaching by quoting part of a verse or passage and leaving the other part out inferring a clear message without actually saying it. It is biblical hinting.

[2]Read Psalm 127:1–5. Note verses 3–5. I love that after the Lord builds the house He speaks of Children as a heritage from God. Our children are a gift!

[3]Matthew 7:27.

[4]Mark 12:29–31.

[5]Scot McKnight, *The Jesus Creed* (Brewster, Mass. Paraclete Press, 2004)

[6]"Christian Moms: Pursue Career or Stay at Home?" http://legacyblog.org/2010/03/08/christian-moms-pursue-career-or-stay-at-home.

[7]Proverbs 31:24.

[8]Proverbs 31:27.

Thoughts for Discussion with Your Spouse or Small Group

1. How does the way you are currently living your life illustrate your definition of success?

2. Are you building your house on the rock or in the sand? Explain.

3. How does your definition of success need to change in order to build a biblical legacy into the life of your child or children?

4. Is there a need for someone in your family to stay home to provide balance and simplicity? What kind of life adjustment would that be for your family?

5. How does paying for, pursuing, maintaining, or using your possessions add to or take away from family time together?

6. Evaluate your family schedule. Is their time for family night? How can you simplify your schedule in order to buy some important time together?

CHAPTER 4

GET READY TO WALK THE PATH

Have you ever been on a killer hike? I am not talking about a walk in the park but instead a monstrosity to be conquered. Some people think hiking is walking two miles on a comfortable day. Not me my friend. If you ever go hiking with me you will likely be pushed beyond what you think you can bear. I like to pick the most difficult path I can find. There is a sick side of me that snickers as I think about leading people to places they think they can't go, knowing that the whining and complaining will likely be followed by puke.

Hike with me, particularly on an Israel trip, and you will learn what it means to "walk the path." The ancient paths are steep. So steep that your legs feel like they are going to explode followed by an odd sensation of complete numbness and the feeling of weight as you simply try and put one foot in front of the other. Jesus must have been incredibly fit because the paths he walked are full of rocks and crags, switchbacks and climbs. By the time you reach the intended destination, you are bloody, soaking wet, and cantankerous. No matter how much water you drink, salt will form on your shirt and hat and will likely be matted on your eyelashes from intense sweating. Your feet will hurt, your knees will ache, and the next day you will be terribly sore. At the same time you will love it, but not if you failed to prepare before you hit the trail.

In a sense the ancient paths of Israel are the best illustration of the legacy path we are going to walk together. This is a journey that requires preparation and some skills everyone can acquire. At first it seems like an impossible journey but once you are on the path you will realize there is no better path than the ancient path.

Parenting our children spiritually along this path is both grueling and exhilarating. It has its ups and downs, definite switchbacks, and rocky crags. We will have to do some work along the way to lead our children on this path. We will likely experience pain that requires endurance. At the end though, we will look back and realize that the best journey requires the most work. I believe the view at the end of the path will be amazing but for parents leading the next generation spiritually, it really is all about the process. In other words, the journey together along the legacy path is actually more important than the summit. In the words of the writer of Hebrews in chapter 12:1, we have to prepare to *"run with endurance the race set before us."* What kind of preparation is required for the legacy path?

HEART CONNECTION

Dr. Richard Ross, professor of youth ministry at Southwestern Baptist Theological Seminary, continually reminds parents of teenagers about the importance of "heart connections" for spiritual parenting. "Relationships are central to making a spiritual impact on children. Children and teenagers tend to embrace parents' faith if parents have heart connections with them."[1] It will not be enough to convey biblical information to your children as you lead them along the legacy path. You will have to do that in the context of relationship. Children and teenagers who have a heart connection with a parent are very likely to be influenced by them. Parents who lose the heart connection in the teenage years are likely to lose their ability to influence spiritually.

As you prepare to guide your child along the legacy path your first order of business is to establish or reconstruct your heart connection with your child. That looks different at different stages of childhood but there are a couple of constants that your children should understand.

- Spend time with them for no other reason than time together. Often the easiest way to rebuild a broken heart connection is to hang out together with no agenda except to know your kid better.

- Physical touch is important. Hug your kids, kiss them on the cheek, give them a high five, and let them know you are for them not against them.

- Words of affirmation are huge. Make sure your child hears you say, "I love you" several times a day. Let them hear that you are proud of them not because of what they accomplish but because of who they are.

- Convey a love through time, words, and touch that supersedes accomplishments, choices, or accolades.

When they know you love them unconditionally whether they succeed or fail, then you have established a heart connection that goes beyond circumstances. This kind of heart connection begins at birth and carries on into adulthood.

No parent is perfect, but paying attention to your relationship is key to being able to lead your child spiritually. You may have great heart connections with your children from which you can build. It is also possible that you have a broken or shattered heart connection. Parents and teenagers easily drift apart relationally if the heart connection is not cultivated daily. If you find yourself in a broken situation I beg you, go to your child in this moment and humble yourself. Tell them where you have gone wrong in the relationship. Seek to reconcile and ask for forgiveness. Then begin again with genuine love and affection conveyed through time, touch, and words. You will be surprised how God can speak to a hardened teenage heart through the words of a humbled and repentant parent. Before you earn the right to tell them of God's love you have to show it to them. Teach them God believes in them before you teach them to believe in God. Biblical truth is always understood best through the conduit of relationship. How is your heart connection with your children? Now is the time to work on it as you prepare to lead them on the legacy path.

> Convey a love through time, words, and touch that supersedes accomplishments, choices, or accolades.

FAITH TALKS

As parents leading our children spiritually we need to learn how to guide them by leading intentional Faith Talks each week. Faith Talk is another way of saying family devotion. A Faith Talk is a time set aside each week for families to gather around the Bible, its application to life, and the worship of Jesus. Faith Talk is the formal way that parents can teach the biblical truths necessary for our children to understand and apply as they progress along the legacy path.

As parents we need a formal platform to train our children biblically. When you think about it, a lot of people have formal platforms in the lives of our children from which they are influenced daily. Their teachers and coaches hold incredible formal platforms in their lives, shaping our children either positively or negatively. The media actually holds a very formal platform, influencing the youth of our culture dramatically. The church also holds a formal platform in your child's life from the pastor to their Sunday School teacher in the realm of spiritual development. Yet tragically, most parents have not established a formal platform in their families to teach the truth of God's Word. If we are the primary faith trainers, why does everyone else hold a formal platform to teach truth (or lies) and influence worldview except you and me?

Ignite a spiritual fire in your home by honoring Christ formally once per week by leading a family worship time.

Faith Talk is the planned conversation that takes place in obedience to the *Sh'ma*. Remember Deuteronomy 6:6–7? *"And these words that I command you today shall be on your heart. You shall teach them diligently to your children, and shall talk of them when you sit in your house, and when you walk by the way, and when you lie down, and when you rise."*

We live in a day when Christian parents really don't even consider having family devotions. For a couple of decades now the church in general has not emphasized the idea of families having conversations around the Scripture nor have we equipped parents for such a task. I think this is one reason Faith Talks are not even a blip on the radar in most Christian households. If we are to raise a generation of kids who become adults madly in love with Christ we will have to worship the King in our living rooms. Our homes have been devoid of the worship of Christ in recent years leading our children to one practical conclusion: Christ is King at church but not at home.

The tide is turning however as ministry leaders regain appreciation for the home as central to the spiritual formation of the next generation. I am excited to see church leaders pushing faith at home by challenging parents to teach their children the Scripture. I pray you attend a church that is learning to partner with parents to disciple children and youth. Ignite a spiritual fire in your home by honoring Christ formally once per week by leading a family worship time.

As with everything hated by the enemy, there are obstacles placed in the way, common to parents who want to lead Faith Talks. Perhaps most common is the busyness of life. After all, there is always another opportunity for at least one member of the family in conflict with Faith Talk each week. You can overcome this obstacle but it will not be easy. It actually will take wisdom and leadership on your part as the leaders of your family. Prioritizing "Faith Talk" means protecting time for the family to talk about the Word and learn how to live God's way. This requires leadership especially as your children get older. Get it on their weekly schedule and make it an expected event. As a parent you will need wisdom to know when you should be flexible on this. There are times that it is perfectly okay to reschedule but that should not be the norm.

A second, very common obstacle is that most parents feel ill equipped to lead a Faith Talk. Sometimes when I talk to parents about Faith Talks their initial reaction is, "Easy for you to say." Their assumption is that either because I went to seminary or because I am a pastor that somehow Faith Talks are easy for me. Their assumption could not be farther from the truth. Faith Talk is a discipline that my wife and I have learned and will continue to learn as our children grow through different phases of life. We are all on a level playing field when it comes to Faith Talks. Like me, unless you had a great parental example, you will have to learn how to lead a Faith Talk. Any parent can do this. God has hard-wired you for faith influence. After reading this next section you will never be able to say, "I don't know how."

HOW TO LEAD A FAITH TALK

Since most of us may have never led a Faith Talk let's start with some baby steps. The best advice I can give you is to start early in your child's life if you have the opportunity. It is much easier to lead Faith Talks for middle school or high school students when the concept has been part of the family spiritual discipline since the day they were born. At the same time, not everyone has this luxury. Most of you likely have children older than infancy. In this case, jump in right where you are. There is no better time than the present.

In our family there are really two kinds of Faith Talks that take place. First is the planned and formal Faith Talk occurring one time per week. Second are intentional but informal Faith Talks that take place almost every day. Let's begin with the planned, weekly Faith Talk.

SCHEDULE

I use the word "formal" to describe this Faith Talk because it is a planned event. As with any planned event, a time must be determined and everyone must agree to attend. We like to use Sunday for our Faith Talk. For our family it makes sense to worship on Sunday morning with our biblical community at church, spend the day together relaxing and playing, and end the day with a Faith Talk. It does not have to be Sunday but you do need to pick a time and stick with it.

CREATE A FESTIVE ENVIRONMENT

When you look back to the Jewish roots of the Christian faith you will find a very special day devoid of work and reserved for God, family, rest, and play called Sabbath. We would do well to learn some lessons from the Sabbath as we think about our own Faith Talks. In the Old Testament, the Sabbath is a day to be celebrated. The rabbi's say the Sabbath comes in with celebration and goes out with mourning. This is a day where people look forward to being with their God and their people. Compare this to your Sunday. What if we purposefully slowed down enough to celebrate God together as families on Sunday? What if Sunday became a day of celebration?

There are some little things we can do here. Light a candle and let it burn all day as a sign that Sunday is different from all the other days. Have a special meal together and linger at the table for conversation signaling that you are in a hurry to go nowhere. After worshiping together at church, do things that the family will enjoy. Somewhere in there have your Faith Talk.

We like to mix it up. We find that it keeps things interesting. We might have lunch together and then watch a movie at home followed by our Faith Talk. Our day might look like worship, a walk to the community pool with Dad while Mom gets some much needed rest, and then Faith Talk at home. Some of our best Faith Talks have been around the table at our local Starbucks. All of that works for my family at this stage in the game. You have to find what works for your unique family in your season of life. Just make it enjoyable instead of bearable.

TEACH TO THEIR PLACE ON THE PATH

In the next chapter you will discover that each of our children is on a different place in their spiritual journey along the legacy path. When we lead Faith Talks we have to teach to their place on the path. As parents that means understanding where each of our children is in their journey. That goes beyond the mechanics of leading a Faith Talk to the heart connection you have with your children and discernment that only God's Spirit can give.

I have friends who have it really easy when it comes to leading Faith Talks that focus on where their children are on the path because they only have one child. I have other friends who have seven children. How difficult is it to lead a Faith Talk that connects with everyone in the family? We have three. How do you lead a Faith Talk that relates well with a middle schooler, and elementary aged child, and a toddler?

The short answer is that you don't. You will never lead a Faith Talk that connects with every child every time. However, God will use what you teach to connect with everyone some of the time. There are times when our Faith Talks are mostly for our three year old and the older girls know it. These look like music with lots of singing and dancing and throwing kids in the air, followed by a shorter biblical theme like "God made me." It may seem simple to our oldest daughter but later we will get to have conversations centered on our identity in light of the fact that God made us as His children.

Your leadership with each of your children goes beyond a weekly Faith Talk. Your Faith Talk will be the launching pad for one-on-one conversations with your children throughout the week focused to their section of the path. Relax about this. It does not have to perfect and everyone does not have to get it every time. God is going to use it anyway because when families gather around His Word He is pleased and He is present.

DISCOVER AGE-APPROPRIATE RESOURCES

It is important to teach Faith Talks that intersect with your child's place along the path as often as possible. Some parents love to do this their own way finding the creative aspect of the challenge fun. They like to use what God is teaching them in the Word and relate it to their kids in a way that helps them move forward in their spiritual growth.

Other parents need help with this. In this case it is very important to discover resources that match the place of your child along the path. For many parents just finding the right tool catapults them into a whole new world of Faith Talks that intentionally teach their children what is necessary to progress spiritually. The problem is parents often find it difficult to know where to find just the right resources. Likely your children's pastor or student pastor will have some great recommendations. Let me also suggest my listing of approved resources that my team has developed and constantly updates for the parents of our church. Visit us at http://www.legacymilestones.com/resources.

DIP INTO YOUR SPIRITUAL TANK

If you attend a church you likely get your "spiritual tank" filled weekly through a pastor's sermon or your small group. A simple way to lead a Faith Talk for your family is to re-teach what you just learned from the sermon or in your Bible study. Obviously those environments are geared for adults. You can take the biblical principles you learn and convey them to your children through your Faith Talks in a way they can understand. For some parents this is the easiest first step. Many churches today are doing some really helpful things to help parents lead Faith Talks. Some pastors actually write Faith Talks based on their current sermon and hand them out or put them on the church website. Many small group Bible studies offer a take-home piece for parents that will help us lead Faith Talks based on what we just learned in small group Bible study. Find out what your church is doing to help parents lead Faith Talks well. You may find that your church is working hard to make your Faith Talk at home successful.

TELL STORIES

A crucial aspect to leading effective Faith Talks is story telling.

Everyone loves a great story, especially kids. You can read the story of David and Goliath or you can tell it as a story. Act out the story. Assign parts. Let someone be Saul, someone be David, find a tall Goliath, and whoever is left can be the army of Israel. Define a valley in your living room or backyard. Put Goliath and the Philistines on one side and Saul, David, and the army of Israel on the other. Let the family playing Goliath step into the valley and challenge the army of Israel as stated in 2 Samuel 17. You get the idea. You can either read the Scripture verbatim or you can tell the story. The story always sticks!

It is also important to tell stories from your own life and faith. When our oldest daughter was seven we took our kids to the local park for the afternoon for some fun time together and our family Faith Talk. After our Faith Talk we decided to tell our kids our own stories of how we came to place our faith in Jesus. Angela told her story and I told mine. The stories made the relationship real to Hailey for the first time. Soon after Hailey made a decision to put her faith in Jesus like only a child can. Our stories were more meaningful and impactful to her than ten Faith Talks. Let your kids see the work of Christ in your life and tell them your story. This is such an important aspect of family Faith Talks.

> Let your kids see the work of Christ in your life and tell them your story.

DAILY FAITH TALKS

There is a second kind of Faith Talk that is just as important and just as intentional. This is Faith Talk that takes place in a less formal, daily, sort of way. This is the rhythm of an intentional ongoing faith conversation between parent and child patterned after the daily rhythm of Deuteronomy 6. Often this daily conversation flows from the content of the formal Faith Talk. Daily conversation gives parents the opportunity to apply truth to each child according to their place on the path. For instance, if we have a formal Faith Talk lesson on the Ten Commandments, we need to apply it in unique ways to our 11 year old, our 8 year old, and our 3 year old. This daily conversation is the answer to the question, "How do I lead Faith Talks if my children are at different places along the legacy path?" You apply the truth one-on-one throughout the week.

GOING TO BED

God knew that 'bedtime" is an important moment daily for faith conversation even as he led Moses to pen the *Sh'ma*. It is why we are told that we should impress the commands of God on our children as we lie down. Bedtime, quite frankly, is a holy moment full of heart connection and conversation. The question is "how to use bedtime for faith talk."

When I am in town, which is most nights, I have the privilege of tucking all three of my girls in bed. I like it because it is Dad's time to reconnect and talk. Right now that looks different with each daughter depending on her age and personality. The common elements include conversation, prayer, blessing, songs, and kisses. I like to ask them about their day. I often ask what the best thing of the day was and what the worst thing of the day was. Some nights this yields no fruit. Other nights I get an earful and learn what life was like for my children while I was at work. I learn about their concerns, fears, hopes, and dreams all in a few minutes per night.

Sometimes I have an agenda for this conversation based on a verse God spoke to me about my daughter. We will talk about the Scripture for a moment and then we pray. We take turns. I love to hear them pray because it tells me about their connection with the Father. I end by praying a biblical blessing over them. There are many blessings that leap right off the pages of Scripture to pray over your children. One such blessing is Aaron's priestly blessing found in Numbers 6:24-26. Reach at your hand and touch your child's back or head and pray, *"The* L̲ord *bless you and keep you; the* Lord *make his face to shine upon you and be gracious to you; the* Lord *lift up his countenance upon you and give you peace."* In this way you bless your child with the very words of God. For a great resource designed to help you learn the blessings of Scripture and to pray them over your child see *A Father's Guide to Blessing His Children* by David Michael available at www.childrendesiringgod.org. Wrap it up with a song and a kiss and you have just used bedtime to lead your child along the legacy path.

In case you are thinking, "Yeah! Sounds great for younger kids, but I have teenagers," let me implore you to think again. I will never forget talking to my former pastor and friend, Alex, about bedtime as an important moment every day with my little ones. He looked at me and said, "That should never change." He went on to tell me that he did the same kind of thing with his children until the day they left for college. Then when they come home for a break, he showed up again at bedtime.

I once heard my friend Dr. Richard Ross, speaking of his son's transition to college. He conveyed that his son said the weirdest thing about the whole deal was bedtime because Dad wasn't there for that important moment of heart connection, blessings, and Faith Talk. Contrary to popular parental belief solid research suggests teenagers are crying out for a deeper relationship with their parents. Show up at bedtime. Your fifteen year old will come to expect their blessing in a few short weeks. You can do this!

GETTING UP

If you have kids in school and you work, mornings are rushed. I totally understand. Our house starts waking up at 6:15 A.M. and we start departing in shifts by 7:30 A.M. At the same time, we find that getting up is an important opportunity to impress the words of God and His love on our children. You are going to have to find your unique way of capitalizing on the "morning" opportunity, but don't miss it.

Most days we grab a few minutes with each of our daughters as they eat breakfast before heading to school. This is our daily attempt to pour truth from God's Word into their life. We use the book of Proverbs, over and over again each month. We use Proverbs because it is easy, it requires minimal prep, and it allows us to follow a schedule. Proverbs has 31 chapters allowing us to utilize a chapter for each corresponding day of the month. We do not read the entire chapter but instead we choose one verse from each chapter. Yesterday I picked a verse out of Proverbs 31 (since it was August 31) and we read it together. I started by making it funny. Proverbs 31:6 says, "*Give strong drink to the one who is perishing, and wine to those in bitter distress.*" Hailey asked, "Are you kidding me?" Madelyn asked, "Do we have any beer dad?" So rule number one: pick a proverb that will speak into their lives. I was just kidding, so we read about the virtuous woman in Proverbs 31:10-31. It was a great opportunity to talk about who they are becoming in the Lord and to also point out how much their mama looks a lot like that Proverbs 31 gal. It is that simple and it takes all of ten minutes.

Angela uses the morning walk to the bus stop to pray with our girls. She gets up early so that she can walk hand and hand with each daughter to the bus as they head out into the world for the day. Sometimes I go with them and listen as my wife bathes her daughters in prayer and blessing.

"Getting up" time is a great opportunity to start the day leading our children to fix their eyes on Jesus. It is important that some of the first words your children and mine consider every morning are the very Words of God. It is not only a great idea but we find that it is part of the normal life rhythm for parents leading their children spiritually every day.

HOW TO CAPTURE GOD MOMENTS

Following the pattern of Deuteronomy 6:4-9 grants parents a simple and yet God-breathed plan for training the next generation. If our planned Faith Talk each week qualifies as "*when you sit in your home*" and our daily Faith Talks cover "*when we lie down, and when we rise,*" then capturing God moments is the art of faith training as we "*walk by the way.*"

"*Walking by the way*" isn't what it used to be. Instead of walking miles from the village into town or leading sheep through the desert, we walk, drive, bike, and fly through life. The point of as you are "*walking by the way*" is as you are traveling through life together. Along the way, whether you are driving, flying, or walking, you will encounter countless opportunities to demonstrate Christian faith and to speak biblical truth into your child's life. It is a matter of learning how to capture "God moments." A God moment is just that: a moment ordained by God designed for parents to speak truth to their children in the midst of normal life situations. These moments are not manufactured but instead captured as they emerge for the purpose of leading our children spiritually.

> A God moment is just that: a moment ordained by God designed for parents to speak truth to their children in the midst of normal life situations.

One night while I was putting my daughter in bed a God moment emerged that changed the course of her life forever. We went through our normal seven year old girl bedtime routine . . . light out, running little girl jumps into my arms as I simultaneously throw her into bed after performing the helicopter . . . conversation, songs, prayers, and a kiss good night. At the end of our routine I expected the normal ritual of "I love you more." Instead, my little girl was crying. I will let you in on a dark secret. I was torn because I could smell the popcorn my wife made and I knew she was downstairs waiting for our nightly "popcorn and T.V. and conversation session." Do I quickly comfort my daughter and then head downstairs before the popcorn was gone or do I capture the God moment; that was the question. I chose to stay as I heard the crunching of popcorn in the background.

I am so glad I did. My daughter began to tell me a story of epic proportions, if you are seven. All year long she had been picked on by a known "mean girl" at school. Toward the end of the school year, let's call it mid-May, my daughter devised a plan to retaliate against the "mean girl." After recess they stood in line next to each other at the water fountain. My daughter went first and splashed herself with water and then told the teacher that the "mean girl" threw water on her. The teacher believed Pastor Brian's daughter and assumed that the "mean girl" had lived up to her reputation. Now it was July and my daughter found herself in bed confessing. She had held this in for almost six weeks.

What came next was truly extraordinary. My daughter and I got to talk about how to recognize the feeling of conviction in our lives. We talked about how God puts that bad feeling in your stomach when you have done something that is wrong. We got to talk about the freedom of confessing our sins to each other and God. We talked about forgiveness and we prayed for God to forgive my daughter for lying. The next day my wife and daughter discussed reconciliation and forgiveness. What do you do when you have hurt someone? So Angela led my daughter to call the "mean girl" and ask her forgiveness and she called her teacher to tell her the truth and seek forgiveness. Both the teacher and the "mean girl" were quick to offer forgiveness. My daughter was free and she learned a valuable lesson that was crucial to her coming salvation. Angela and I recognized the work of the Holy Spirit in her life as she confessed her sin without us compelling her to do so. The God moment was the beginning of the path leading to her salvation and baptism (Milestone 2).

We need a couple of things in order to capture God moments and speak truth into them.

- We need a presence. You cannot capture God moments if you are not with your children when they happen. Sometimes people think God moments are the easy part of this plan. I tend to disagree. You may have to rearrange your entire life to capture God moments. Are you with your children as you walk by the way? We also need wisdom to see God moments and to know what to say when they happen. James 1:5 says, "*If any of you lacks wisdom, let him ask God, who gives generously to all without reproach, and it will be given him.*"

- We need to beg God for wisdom to recognize and capture the God moments in life. Angela (my wife) and I make this a consistent practice of our personal prayer lives. "Lord, grant us the wisdom to see the God moments and the direction of your Spirit to speak into them for the bolstering of faith in the lives of our children."

A working knowledge of Faith Talks and God moments arms us with the skills necessary to begin the journey. Everything you have read to this point is necessary to guide your children spiritually. Take time now to reflect on what you have read. You understand the theology, you seek to abide in Christ, you are making the changes to build your house on the rock, and you are ready to lead Faith Talks and capture God moments. Now, let's walk the path of legacy milestones.

ENDNOTES

[1]Richard Ross, *Student Ministry and the Supremacy of Christ* (Bloomington, Indiana: Crossbooks, 2009), 163.

———————

Thoughts for Discussion with Your Spouse or Small Group

1. How is your heart connection with your children? Spend some time describing your relationship with each child. Do you connect better with some than others?

2. How can you improve your heart connection with each of your children?

3. Discuss a time for a weekly Faith Talk that would work best for your family. Go ahead and schedule your first Faith Talk. Let your family know what you are planning to do and lead them to guard the time.

4. What can you do beginning tomorrow to lead your children spiritually when they go to bed and when they get up? Be intentional about leading them spiritually tonight.

5. Remember a God moment that you have already experienced with your child. How can you capture more God moments as you walk along the road?

6. What part should prayer play in your Faith Talks and God moments?

CHAPTER 5

THE PATH OF LEGACY MILESTONES

MILESTONES 1–3: FOUNDATIONAL FAITH DESTINATIONS FOR CHILDREN

This may sound grotesque, but I wish a handbook came connected to the umbilical chord of each child as she is born into the world. How cool would that be? A playbook from God describing exactly how He would like us to parent this new life. A unique owner's manual describing how the child is wired so we know how to lead her spiritually. It doesn't happen that way though. Instead, we drive away from the hospital 48 hours later, after having passed the car seat test, expected to know how to parent our new son or daughter. Parenthood levels the playing field. Professional status, earned degrees, income, and perceived success aside every Christian parent drives away from the hospital feeling baffled and wishing they had a road map for effective spiritual training among other things.

Instead we get Proverbs 22:6. *"Train up a child in the way he should go; even when he is old he will not depart from it."* I am grateful for the wise truth contained in this Scripture. I'll be honest though. As a new parent, I needed a little more. I was thinking, "Great, but please tell me how to train up a child in the way he should go." Of course there is a lot more in Scripture on that very topic.[1] The emerging biblical plan for parenting our children for legacy is best illustrated by a simple path. Why a path? A path is indicative of a journey. A path is simple: it goes in an intentional direction, and it is best experienced with a guide who understands the destination and has walked the path before. Certainly a path affords varying degrees of adventure, joy, scenic overlooks, and treacherous terrain along the way. Along the path are points of measurement that indicate progress like mile markers or kilometer markers along the highway. We will call these points, legacy milestones.

A milestone is an event, preceded by a period of instruction from parents, which celebrates a spiritual development point in a child's life.[2] "The legacy path consists of seven milestones that every person, growing in his or her relationship with Christ, should experience and celebrate. These milestones serve as markers of progression in the spiritual formation journey. When a milestone is reached, growth is celebrated as praise for how God is working in the person and as motivation to continue walking the path."[3] The beauty of milestones is that they are natural and normal growth points along the way as a person grows in Christ. As a parent you really don't have to manufacture anything. You simply follow Christ along the path and lead your children to do the same in a very intentional way. Legacy Milestones is an intentional plan for parenting children who grow into adult Christ-followers.

KNOW WHERE YOU ARE AND WHERE YOU ARE GOING

Several years ago, after traveling and studying in Israel, I began to guide trips, teaching the Bible and exploring the land associated with much of the Text. The thing is, I am not the type of guy who can just ride a bus around, get out and teach, and then board the bus again to drive to the next destination. I want the people who go with me to "KNOW" the land of the Bible. I want to put them in the footsteps of Jesus to hear His voice as He led His disciples along the ancient paths. So we hike up hills, down hills, through the desert, along the beach, and in the mountains next to the borders of countries such as Egypt, Syria, Lebanon, and Jordan. The problem for a newbie guide is that in order to lead a trip that way, he has to know where he is, where he is going and why he is going there. If he doesn't know where he is and where he is going he is likely to wander aimlessly.

The same is true in parenting. We need to know where we are, where we are going, and why we are going there. Have you thought this through? Maybe it is time to chart your course. Planning your journey is the difference between hoping your kids randomly end up loving God versus actually "training them up in the way they should go." When you do your part you can rest in the wisdom of Proverbs 22:6. Let's take time now to understand the path of legacy milestones. Think of it as a roadmap for the journey of training your kids spiritually. Ask yourself, where are my kids on this path?

MILESTONE 1: BABY DEDICATION

When we had our first daughter, Angela and I were twenty-six years old. In the nine-month time frame leading up to Hailey's birthday, Angela's motherly instinct kicked in. From the beginning I realized God had granted her a keen ability as a mother to understand our daughter and parent her well. As a Dad, of a girl nonetheless, I found myself an emotional mess. I remember thinking, "Pastors all of my life have been teaching me that as a man, I am the spiritual leader of my family." I wondered how I would lead if I didn't know where to go. Several months later we received a letter from my pastor inviting us to participate in a formal "baby dedication" ceremony on a Sunday in November. "We can do that," I thought to myself.

> Planning your journey is the difference between hoping your kids randomly end up loving God versus actually "training them up in the way they should go."

Likely the church you attend practices a form of baby dedication based on its own tradition. The idea of infant dedication flows from the Hebrew context of Scripture.[4] Although most of us don't practice infant dedication in exactly the same way as our Hebrew counterparts, the intent is similar. In an act of worship we are giving back this child that has so graciously been entrusted to us and we are committing to lead her in the "discipline and instruction of the Lord."[5] That is no small act or commitment. I believe this beautiful moment carries with it an act of covenantal promise much like a wedding. In an act of celebration and commitment we vow before our spiritual family and friends to steward the life of our child in a godly way. Our church in turn agrees to partner with us as we help our children grow into adults who love God and love people the way Jesus does.

CORE COMPETENCY

With every milestone come one or more core competencies we as parents must teach our children before they reach the next milestone.

A core competency is an important truth that must be learned and practiced as people progress toward the next milestone. The secret of milestone one is that the core competency is for the parents, not for the child. Likely the child will never remember the event but parents will be impacted by it for a lifetime. The core competency here is elementary but monumental: you are the primary faith trainer by design.

It is interesting that we don't have a choice. Being the primary faith trainer is a mantle of every parent. By design God innately places within a child a soul to be influenced by his parents. It doesn't matter if you are present and involved or disconnected and absent. Parents make disciples by virtue of being mom or dad. As a parent you are making disciples. The question is what kind of disciples you are making?

Recently I met with a twelve year old whose parents divorced when he was three. His mother is a committed Christ-follower. His father is a skeptic. He lives with his mother and spends the majority of his days with her. However, his father, who rarely sees him, has powerful influence over the boy's trust in God. Do you know why? His father, though absent and skeptical, was wired by God to be the primary faith influencer in his son's life. Naturally, the son considers the spiritual life of his absent, skeptical father, as he is becoming a man.

The same is true in the positive sense. When we connect with the fact that God has tied the souls of parents and children together giving parents an incredible influence over their children, we realize our key role in this legacy project. As parents we have the opportunity to be used by God to demonstrate authentic faith and practical Christianity as the next generation grows up in our own homes. What an amazing responsibility and what an incredible opportunity to change the world, one child at a time! Milestone one teaches us that we are the primary faith influencers of our children, even before the church, which by the way is our greatest partner on the legacy path.

AN IMPORTANT REALITY

It is not enough to understand that we are the primary faith influence in the life of our child. We have to move beyond understanding to commitment. In all of the excitement of bringing a new baby home and thinking about who he will become, we sometimes imagine Christian parenting like a trip to Disney World. Sounds like a lot of fun as we dream of magical family moments when our daughters become princesses and our sons become knights in shining armor. Those moments will be there. The journey however is joyous but difficult. It will not be perfect. You will have wonderful days and horrible days and all in between. You will be proud, disappointed, in love, afraid, angry, and simply at a loss. The legacy path, beginning with milestone one, lasts a lifetime. The commitment to be the primary faith trainer is magnificent and horrifying at the same time. Our great hope is in God, the perfect Father.

FAMILY CELEBRATION

We need to learn to party! If you study the Old Testament you will find that God mandates seasons of jubilant celebration as part of His plan for developing the faith of His people. Some translations of the Bible call these celebrations holy convocations and others call them feasts or festivals. These feasts served to help God's people remember His work in their lives and His position and authority as God. The celebration included important family gatherings and massive community gatherings. As Christ-followers we should celebrate the Lord and His work in our lives. Celebrations cement in our minds and hearts the good work of the Lord as we grow spiritually. With every milestone comes an important celebration and milestone one is no different.

Let me make a suggestion. Keep it simple. Often the best celebrations are the ones that are not stressful in preparation. Join in your church's baby dedication ceremony. The church will do much of the work for you. Our church celebrates the commitment by sharing the meaning of the baby's name and presenting parents with a certificate and a photo to remember the commitment. Invite your family and friends to come and witness your commitment to lead your child spiritually and partner with you as your biblical community. Then invite a few close friends or family to your home for a meal. It does not have to be an ordeal. Grill hamburgers if you want. If hosting people at your house freaks you out pick your favorite restaurant. Work together with your spouse to write a short prayer for your new baby at the very beginning of his spiritual journey. Take time during your meal with family and friends to read the prayer and ask them to join you in this prayer of faith.

START A MILESTONES BOX[6]

Start a milestones box. This is a great time to purchase, build, or create a special box for your child to keep important milestone mementos. On my first trip to Israel I picked up handcrafted boxes for my girls to keep the things necessary for them to look back and remember their journey along the path of legacy milestones. Be creative and do something unique for your family, but get them something to help them remember their journey with Christ. Imagine a day that they will leave home and take the box with them. Inside they will find evidence of their own experience as you lead them spiritually. The first thing you put in the box is the prayer you wrote for your son or daughter as you celebrated milestone one. Imagine them, as they prepare for their own children, looking back at the box and remembering how you led them. I can't wait to see a generation of adults whose parents understood their role of primary faith influencers beginning at milestone one! Imagine the legacy! Dream about it as you enjoy your baby and celebrate the first milestone. Some time will go by before you celebrate milestone two.

MILESTONE 2: FAITH COMMITMENT

Do you remember when you began teaching your children to swim? At first our kids were horrified of the water but they trusted Angela and me. This summer we have been teaching our youngest who seems especially timid. One day we made the trek to our community pool. The older girls bolted for the water but Eden stood still at the edge of the pool just looking. She waited for me to get in and then she hesitantly jumped into my arms. As parents we all pray for the time that our children will grow spiritually enough to make a faith commitment of their own. In a way, though we have been praying, teaching, and blessing them along the way, their faith commitment is like jumping into the pool all on their own for the very first time without us standing there to catch them. We play a part in leading them to milestone two, but this one is between them and God.

Somewhere between the ages of about seven and thirteen, children growing up in a Christian home and in the church come to an age where they are able to make a personal decision about their faith in Jesus. There is a reason it is called a "personal decision." We cannot make it for them.

We can pray for them, we can teach them the Scripture, we can share the Gospel, and we can tell them our own stories of salvation but we cannot surrender to Christ for them. The beauty of a love relationship with God is that it is never forced or earned. We do well to remember this as we lead our children toward milestone two.

What constitutes the salvation of a child? Actually it is the same thing that solidifies the faith of any person placing complete trust in Christ. Here's the bad news. As your life and mine prove, we are all sinners. Every last one of us is imperfect and at least occasionally, willfully chooses wrong over right. This sin is a massive problem for God because He is perfectly righteous. His very nature will not allow Him to overlook sin. Instead He, while head over heels in love with us, must judge sin. The Scripture says that the penalty or judgment of our sin is death. The good news is the story does not end there; it really only begins.

Our God is an amazing Father. He loves His kids despite their sin. Not only does His character cause God to impose judgment on sin, His love drives Him to redeem what has been tainted. The Bible says that God so loved us that He sent His Son (Jesus) that whoever believes in Him (Jesus) would have life that lasts forever. It goes on to say that the good news is we can surrender to life in Christ. If we confess with our mouth Jesus is Lord and believe in our heart God raised Him from the dead we will be saved. When a child believes and confesses he is saved and begins a new life in Christ, he needs to comprehend some things. He needs to understand just enough and exercise faith on his own to experience salvation.

CORE COMPETENCIES

Before a child can make a legitimate faith commitment he must understand some things. Don't get me wrong. He doesn't need to understand everything. Just the basics required for salvation. These "basics" are the core competencies for milestone two. Biblically, salvation involves three basic actions: repentance, confession and belief. Repentance is the action of changing directions, turning from sin to Jesus and walking a different way. Confession is the act of agreeing "out-loud." Confession means you not only privately believe Jesus is Lord but you confess it with your words. Confession is agreeing with the true pathway of salvation in and through Jesus the Messiah. Believing is more than just hoping in a story. Romans 10:9 says, "*because if you confess with your mouth that Jesus is Lord and believe in your heart that God raised him from the dead, you will be saved.*" "Believe" in this verse is easily translated as "trust in" which carries a more correct meaning in our use of the English language. Sometimes when we say "believe in" we mean like believing in Santa Claus or the tooth fairy. To "trust in" means to stake all of your hope in the fact that salvation comes through Jesus just as God promised.

So what does a person have to understand in order to repent, believe, and confess? I think every child needs to learn simple biblical truth about Jesus, faith, the Bible, sin, repentance, and salvation. No one comes to Christ knowing everything. In fact we are encouraged to come to God with a simple "child like faith." Still a child needs to understand these things in order to make a legitimate decision to follow Christ.

If you are involved in a church with a Children's Ministry or a Student Ministry driven by the Bible they will learn these concepts there. More effectively, you can teach your children these concepts as you lead Faith Talks at home. What you say and how you live as the primary faith influence will have a definite impact on your child's faith commitment.

NOT A BOX TO HURRY AND CHECK OFF!

Most Christian parents dream of the day their child will make a personal decision to follow Christ. After all, what would we want more than to know that our child is secure in her relationship with God no matter what? Not that this will be a problem for you but it is worth mentioning. Some parents are so anxious to lead their children to salvation that they carefully manufacture a faith commitment. It happens like this. We teach them to parrot the right answers and then help them to memorize the "magic words" so they can get into heaven. Then we march them down the aisle in church or into the pastor's office and say, "My daughter prayed to receive Christ." Remember, salvation is the work of the Holy Spirit and not the manipulation of a well-intentioned parent. Don't rush to celebrate milestone two. Instead lead your child gently using Faith Talks, God moments, and Church and watch as God works in his life.

As a parent what is your cue that God is at work in your child's life? Angela and I have now had the privilege of leading two of our three children to Christ. We have been careful to let the Spirit lead. We have noticed a couple of key indicators that God is working our children toward salvation.

Often our first indicator is an onslaught of questions about Jesus, heaven, hell, baptism, and "how to have Jesus inside" to quote a seven year old. These questions tell the story of a child seeking to know God and her position with Him. Questions are evidence of parents who are teaching their children to ask the right questions, churches who are partnering with parents, and the work of the Holy Spirit. When our children begin to ask us questions we need to take our cue, giving biblical answers in an age-appropriate way.

True conviction comes at the prompting of the Holy Spirit. Conviction demonstrates that we recognize sin and understand that it distances us from God spiritually. Conviction is good because it tells us when we are out of sorts with God and need to repent and come back to Him. This is God's way of calling us back. When you see your child experiencing conviction without your prompting you can know that God is at work.

Finally, un-coerced repentance is a key indication that God is at work in your child's life. It is impossible to repent without knowing your sin and choosing to turn away from it and back toward God and His way of living. We need to recognize this in our child's life when it happens as a sign of heart change even in the most beautiful of hearts. We have a three year old with a beautiful heart. However, repentance is an act of parental coercion in her life at the moment. It will not always be that way. One day she will sense true conviction and experience real repentance in a child-like way. That will be our cue that she is getting closer to milestone two. We won't rush it. We will pray, and teach, demonstrate, and lead all the while watching for God to do His work. Don't be in a hurry to check this box off.

FAMILY CELEBRATION

When a child does experience salvation it is absolutely time to celebrate the continued work of Christ and the child's response to Jesus the King. Milestone two family celebrations easily correspond with the public confession of faith celebrated in local churches. Often baptism is both the church celebration and the family celebration of salvation.[7] Baptism is an excellent picture of what has already happened in a person's life as she repented of her sin and turned her life to Jesus. It also serves as a very public confession that Jesus Christ is Lord.

On the day of the baptism parents invite extended family and friends who have influenced their son or daughter spiritually to celebrate new life in Christ. Then after church, parents may choose to host a spiritual birthday party for their child. Obviously this needs to be done in an age-appropriate way. Seven year olds may love a spiritual birthday cake while older children and teenagers connect better with something else. You decide. You design the celebration. At the spiritual birthday party family members and friends are instructed to bring cards that contain hand written prayers, blessings, or words of encouragement and dependence on Christ. The idea is to create an environment that is fun, memorable, and focused on celebrating the journey to salvation and baptism and life ahead with Christ.

One of the greatest things parents can do at the family celebration is to give the child a gift as a symbol of her new life in Christ. I have seen parents offer many different types of symbols. We gave our girls a sterling cross on a leather strap that is to remind them of their life in Christ because of His saving work on the cross. To this day our girls wear them often to school and to church. When I see the inexpensive necklace adorning their neck I know they had to think about their salvation in Jesus at least for a second. When they are not wearing the crosses, they keep them in their milestone boxes. Our hope is that one day our girls will pass this symbol on to their own children, our grandchildren, as they celebrate a personal faith commitment. Milestone two, salvation and baptism, is the launching pad to the rest of the path and essential to passing a legacy of faith in Christ to the next generation. The legacy path is utterly dependent on the next generation making a very personal commitment to faith in Christ.

MILESTONE 3: PREPARING FOR ADOLESCENCE

The parenting game begins to change at milestone three. No longer are our kids so childlike. Now they are quickly growing and changing physically, spiritually and emotionally. At this stage wise parents are learning to adjust their strategy a bit understanding that their child is progressing toward adolescence. Here our kids begin to form their own opinions, think for themselves, and make choices that up to this point have not been theirs to make. Between the ages of 9 and 12 we parents should intentionally equip our children for the teen years as Christ-followers. Leading children through the turbulent waters of pre-adolescence requires parents to rethink how they connect with their children relationally in order to lead them spiritually. That important heart connection gives us the influence we need to continue leading them spiritually as they grow up.

CORE COMPETENCIES

What do we need to teach our children as they prepare for adolescence? The basics are about helping changing kids navigate relevant issues such as identity in Christ, spiritual growth and disciplines, and physical changes as part of God's plan. We teach these concepts in the context of Faith Talks, relevant God Moments, and the conversation of everyday life. Sometimes, faith training becomes more difficult in early adolescence. You may find that it is harder work. That, my friend, is because your intentionality is now more important than ever.

You have to talk to your children about their changing body and emotions. This is one subject that is dangerous to sweep under the rug. When you are eleven you look at yourself in the mirror and wonder who is looking back. Your emotions run with highs and lows that you never have experienced before. When you are eleven it would be nice if someone explained what is going on. If possible, Mom should take the lead on this with daughters and dads with sons. At the same time both parents should be ready, available, and intentional about addressing puberty issues.

> Leading children through the turbulent waters of pre-adolescence requires parents to rethink how they connect with their children relationally in order to lead them spiritually.

Some thoughts here: since our changing bodies are such a normal part of life we need to talk about it in normal ways. Stop the panic, knock off the awkward looks, stop shushing questions about private parts or sex, and start talking about all of that in light of God's plan. Does that horrify you? As a dad of three daughters I have learned to make it normal because at first, I was making it awkward mostly because of my own issues. If you want to be the people your kids turn to when it comes to relationships and sex, communicate normally with them about everything in the puberty category. If at this point they sense from you any bit of shame associated with their changing body or any hint that sex is dirty instead of a wonderful part of God's plan, you lose them. This is so hard for parents but such an easy and freeing line of communication. Start talking with your kids about sex before they start asking questions. In our culture that means ages ten or eleven is probably too late.

When my youngest daughter was two she asked about her private parts like most two year olds do. My wife said, "Oh that hole is made by God. He put it there so that when you get married you can have babies." My two year old was satisfied and my wife began to lay the groundwork for a biblical worldview concerning sex and our bodies. In that one sentence she taught our little girl that God designed her private parts for the specific purpose of having babies in the context of marriage. This was a pretty simple and a very intentional beginning of a conversation that will continue through young adulthood with our daughter. This is not a one-time conversation but an open line of communication.

We make a mistake when we think milestone three is all about "the talk." If you only have one talk you will fail miserably at leading them in this area of their life. There are many great, biblically based resources out there to help you learn how to communicate with your preteen and build the heart connection necessary to make these issues part of how you lead them spiritually.[8]

Milestone three is not all about puberty and sex. I emphasize it here because I believe parents do not realize the importance of their influence over this area of development. This is "the" time to teach our growing children more about their identity in Christ.

I served as a youth pastor for a number of years. One of the things I always noticed about our kids is that they are constantly seeking to define themselves. They want to answer the question, "Who am I?" Leading our children toward milestone three has a lot to do with helping them discover their identity. We will have to do this throughout adolescence but the pre-teen years are an excellent time to begin helping them answer the question, "Who am I?" The answer to this question is rooted in a person's understanding of his position with God. It sounds complicated but when a child knows who God is he will know who he is foundationally. Why is this true? The Scripture says that God made man in His own image.[9] The Bible also says that as Christ-followers we are to be conformed to the image of His Son.[10] So our identity quandary begins to crystallize as we see God as our Creator/Father who loves His creation/kids. Out identity crystallizes even more when we realize that as God's kids we are being molded into the likeness of His Son, Jesus. Why is this important and why now?

The world tells our children lies about who they are . . . especially in adolescence. The culture whispers, "Life is all about you" when in reality life is all about God and His story through us. A child who believes the world revolves around him will make decisions as a teenager that serve to exalt self. I believe Western individualism is the great identity crisis our children face in the 21st century. When it's all about you then you will have sex before marriage. When it is all about you then you will get divorced when things are difficult. When it is all about you then you will spend money you don't have on material possessions to find happiness. When your identity is in yourself then you get to define yourself and this is a tragic mistake. I know a lot of 40 year olds who are still trying to "find themselves."

On the other hand when your identity is in Christ, then you begin to make life choices based on a biblical worldview even as a teenager. When you realize that you were created in the image of God, bought with the price of the blood of Jesus on the cross, and are now being conformed to the likeness of Christ, life has a very different perspective. When faced with the opportunity to have sex before marriage likely you consider that you are being conformed to Christ. When faced with the opportunity to pursue a life solely to accumulate wealth you are likely to consider that Jesus said our purpose is to love God and love people. When you grow up and your marriage becomes difficult you are likely to rely on your Creator to help you through.

A biblical worldview changes everything. As a parent you give your child the gift of understanding his position with God as a Christ-follower when you intentionally teach him about his identity in Christ. Your child is one of God's favorite kids. His Spirit will work in your child. As a parent He will use you to bring about that growth as you intentionally teach your preteen about her identity in Christ. Leading our children to understand their identity in Christ also demands we teach them how to pursue Christ on their own. To this point it is possible their prayer life has always been in partnership with you. It could be that their Bible reading has been led by you up until now. Leaving a legacy means teaching our children how to pursue God and grow in Him when we are not around. Central core competencies for milestone three culminate in personal spiritual growth and spiritual discipline. To me, this means we need to teach our children to pray and to follow God by studying the Scriptures daily . . . on their own.

We have to show them how to do this. It is not enough to just expect it. You have probably been modeling prayer for them since the day they were born. Keep praying with them as much as you can throughout the day. Go beyond that and teach them to pray themselves in their personal alone times with God. Show them how to read the Bible devotionally. We are finding our girls do well with this as we provide tools that guide them through a personal time with God. You may want to help them by getting them a devotional Bible designed for their age or a devotional guide they can use to help them read the Scripture for life application. Show them what you do. If you have a journal you keep as you read the Bible and pray, show it to them. Let them read it. They need to see how you do it. Have a quiet time with them for a week and model time alone with God your way. It sounds easy but this demonstration of spiritual discipline is missing in most Christian families. What would it be like if the next generation learned to read the Bible and pray daily by watching their parents and learning from them? Let's be those parents!

FAMILY CELEBRATION

The culmination of Milestone three is a family celebration called "Road Trip." The purpose of the road trip is to facilitate a fun weekend between father and son or mother and daughter if the family structure allows. The road trip involves connecting with the child relationally around something she enjoys. Along the way, you can use the drive time to talk about specific issues such as changing body parts, puberty, emotions, and the importance of making choices that honor God. Realistically this is not a "cold turkey" conversation. The conversational aspect of the road trip is effective only as it pours out of months of family devotions and discussions leading up to Milestone 3.

Recently my wife took our oldest daughter on her "Road Trip." They planned a trip together to The Woodlands, a community just North of Houston. Hailey's excitement about the road trip heightened as the time grew closer and closer. They made the hour long trek to a hotel where they stayed together overnight before a day of walking around a neat shopping area, waterway, and all around cool place. Hailey got to choose her favorite restaurant and even order dessert afterwards, which for us is a really big deal. Angie and Hailey had a really great time but with a clear purpose. Angela used the time to have very important conversation with Hailey about her changing body, sex, and her identity in Christ. They made a memory with a purpose. For some parents the whole idea of a weekend like this is scary. There are some tools out there I think will prepare you well and that you can actually use with your preteen on your weekend away. I have done the work of identifying and reviewing those resources for you.[11]

"The beauty of milestone three lies in the extent to which the family and the church work together to help a child prepare for adolescence spiritually and emotionally. So often kids have to work through all of this on their own without a model or a relational connection to an adult."[12] As a parent deeply committed to hurling godly legacy into the next generation you can prepare your child for adolescence as a Christ-follower in the 21st century.

ENDNOTES

[1]Deuteronomy 6:4–9, Psalm 78:1–8, Proverbs 22:6, Matthew 22:37–40, Mathew 28:18-20, Ephesians 6:4.

[2]Jim Weidmann, *Spiritual Milestones: A Guide to Celebrating Your Children's Spiritual Passages* (Colorado Springs: Cook Communications, 2001), 10.

[3]Brian Haynes, *Shift: What it Takes to Finally Reach Families Today* (Loveland,

Colorado: Group Publishing, 2009), 42.

[4]Luke 2:21–22 depicts Mary and Joseph participating in the required ceremony of naming, purification, and dedication where our baby dedication ceremonies find their root.

[5]Ephesians 6:4.

[6]Not every family begins at milestone 1. You can start a milestone box wherever you begin your journey as a family. Don't think this is just for milestone one. It is for the entire path.

[7]Obviously there are different church traditions related to baptism. My purpose here is not to argue for one type of baptism or another but instead to broadly show how many people celebrate salvation. You are the primary faith trainer and can adjust your family celebration to correspond with your theological tradition.

[8]For a complete listing of suggested resources visit www.legacymilestones. com/milestone3resources.

[9]Genesis 1:27.

[10]Romans 8:29.

[11]www.legacymilestones.com/milestone3resources.

[12]Brian Haynes, *Shift: What it Takes to Finally Reach Families Today* (Loveland, Colorado: Group Publishing, 2009), 69.

Thoughts for Discussion with Your Spouse or Small Group

1. Think about your younger kids. Where are they on the legacy path? Where do they need to go next?

2. How will you lead your younger children to the next milestone using Faith Talks and God moments?

3. How do you see God working in your child's life even now?

4. What changes do you need to make in your personal life and family life in order to guide your younger children along the legacy path?

5. Where will you go to find resources that will help you lead Faith Talks teaching the appropriate core competencies for your child's place on the legacy path?

CHAPTER 6

THE JOURNEY FROM ADOLESCENCE TO ADULTHOOD

LEGACY MILESTONES 4–7

My wife and I are just entering this phase of parental leadership with our oldest daughter. What you are about to get is our plan, not our parental experience. At the same time, I bring to the table countless hours of study on top of years as a youth pastor and a family pastor observing the good, the bad, and the ugly of helping a child grow spiritually through the teenage years into a vibrant life in Christ as an adult. I think I have seen it all in fifteen years. I have observed Christian parents who do it all right and their kids become spiritual giants as adults. I have observed Christian parents who do it right and their kids become prodigals as adults. I know parents who did it all wrong and somehow by God's grace, their children overcame tremendous obstacles to become amazing adults. I have seen Christian parents do it all wrong and their kids become adults who do it all wrong with zeal. At the end of the day, our children become adults who get to choose their way of life. Hang on to Proverbs 22:6. In the end wisdom says, they will follow their training.

Perhaps the most common scenario in Christian parenting during the teen years is the "I will get them in a good youth ministry and hope they turn out all-right" approach. In this scenario the Christian parent abdicates his responsibility of spiritual leadership to a youth pastor who may be trying to spiritually parent fifty or more students in about three hours a week. Can you imagine trying to parent fifty teenagers while only spending three hours a week with them? That is clearly impossible.

As parents, sometimes in an effort to let our kids grow up or offer more freedom and responsibility or maybe just to keep the peace, we negate our role as primary faith trainers. I think adolescence to adulthood is the season our children need our influence and guidance more than ever. So how can we lead them along the path of legacy milestones as children approaching biblical manhood and womanhood?

MILESTONE 4: COMMITMENT TO PURITY

Being the primary faith trainer of a teenager is no easy role. I have learned well from others that two things really matter here: relational connection and open lines of communication. Relationship and communication earn us the right to teach our students in formal and informal ways. If we lead well as parents, by the age of thirteen our new teenagers should be equipped with everything they need to make a biblical commitment to purity for life. This is more than a commitment ceremony in your local church. Milestone four is about spending the time and energy necessary to disciple them around the core competencies of biblical purity, healthy relationships, and once again, identity in Christ.

We have been commissioned to raise teenagers who become Christ-following adults in this cultural context. Clearly a predominant influencer in our culture is sexuality as the world presents it. As parents it is our job to demonstrate what it means to be biblically pure, first with our own lives and relationships, and then by the teaching of our children. In order to lead well we need to understand the culture. Recent studies suggest that many Christian parents believe their teenagers are not sexually active instead regarding sexual activity before marriage as a problem that other families face. Christian parents aimlessly wander into this trap taking a "holier than thou" approach to the influence our sexualized culture has on our children. None of us can afford to stick our heads in the sand on this one.

Consider the statistics: according to the Center of Disease Control, in 2009, 46% of high school students had ever had sexual intercourse, and 14% of high school students had had four or more sex partners during their life. In 2009, 34% of currently sexually active high school students did not use a condom during their last sexual intercourse. In 2002, 11% of males and females aged 15-19 had engaged in anal sex with someone of the opposite sex; 3% of males aged 15-19 had had anal sex with a male. In 2002, 55% of males and 54% of females aged 15-19 had engaged in oral sex with someone of the opposite sex. In 2006, an estimated 5,259 young people aged 13-24 in the 33 states reporting to CDC were diagnosed with HIV/AIDS, representing about 14% of the persons diagnosed that year. Each year, there are approximately 19 million new STD infections, and almost half of them are among youth aged 15 to 24. In 2002, 12% of all pregnancies, or 757,000, occurred among adolescents aged 15-19.[1]

It is possible to view these statistics from both the positive and the negative perspective. Glass half-full parents might say a relatively small percentage of teenagers are doing the really bad things. A pessimistic parent might say all teenagers are having sex these days and there is nothing we can do. The truth lies somewhere in the middle but let me point out two things. First according to the above report from the CDC, almost half of all high school students have had sex at least once as of 2009. As of 2002, which was a few years ago, over half of male and female high school students had engaged in oral sex. Basically, not scientifically, about half of all high school students are engaged in what the Bible would call "sexual immorality and impurity."[2] Add the issue of pornography to the biblical immorality category and you will find the culture seems to be winning the battle for the purity of our teenaged sons and daughters. Needless to say, it is likely some of these statistics represent teenagers who also call themselves Christian. Some suggest there is no difference between religious teenagers and teenagers claiming no religion when it comes to decisions about sexual morality.

CORE COMPETENCIES

For a long time Christian parents, mostly following the lead of the church, viewed the subject of "sex" as an awkward issue not to be discussed. In many Christian homes, the topic of sex was reduced to one "birds and the bees" talk by Mom or Dad. For years we have laughed at movies and stories depicting just this scenario. In truth it is a joke to think one conversation is enough. Leading up to milestone four we need to have many conversations around the core competencies of biblical purity, biblical sex, healthy relationships, and identity in Christ.

Faith talks and God moments will provide countless opportunities for conversation between milestone three and four.

What should you talk about in Faith Talks? Most parents dread these conversations but the Scripture speaks clearly on the subject of our sexuality. One of the best things you can do as you lead your child toward this milestone is to study the Scripture for yourself and determine what resources out there will give you helpful ideas for Faith Talks. Let me suggest a few organized by the core competencies associated with milestone four.

BIBLICAL PURITY

Our teenagers need to understand that purity is multi-dimensional. It is not just physical but it is also mental, emotional, and spiritual. In our culture we easily justify impurity by compartmentalizing. For instance, a teenager may think it's ok to look at pornography because he is not really doing anything physically with another person. Therefore, he is not hurting anyone. This could not be farther from the truth. Sexual sin is the only sin that is clearly identified as destructive to the mind, spirit, and body. First Corinthians 6:18 says, *"Flee from sexual immorality. Every other sin a person commits is outside the body, but the sexually immoral person sins against his own body."* God has a better plan aimed at avoiding immorality, instead pursuing purity. First Thessalonians 4:3-5 says, *"For this is the will of God, your sanctification: that you abstain from sexual immorality; that each one of you know how to control his own body in holiness and honor, not in the passion of lust like the Gentiles who do not know God."* God's plan for our lives is purity of heart, mind, and soul. This allows us to stay in a right relationship with Him and separates our way of living from every other person in the world. In short, we are God's people and the proof is in our purity. Our children need to understand God's expectation for their sanctification is on a different plane than the average Joe. We are God's kids and He expects us to live as such.

How can a young man or woman keep his way pure in this day and age? It may seem impossible, but it is not. Can I bust a myth for you? We do not live in the only sexually immoral culture that has ever existed. Don't get me wrong. There are atrocities that go on in our culture every day and Satan is doing his job to pervert God's plan for sexual pleasure.

We are on a downward slide morally, but it has been this bad before. Throughout the ages Christians have struggled to remain pure in the face of culturally accepted immorality. Your family must do the same. A young man or woman can keep his or her way pure in 21st century Western civilization. I know some amazing teenagers who are doing just that.

One day Jesus took His disciples on quite a field trip. STOP NOW and read the account in Matthew 16:13-20 and Mark 8:27-38. Don't bypass the Scripture or you will miss the point here. If you read closely you will observe that Jesus marches His young disciples from a small village near the Sea of Galilee called Bethsaida more than 20 miles north to a Roman spa called Caesarea of Philippi. These young Jewish boys from the very conservative "triangle area" of Galilee were headed to the proverbial den of iniquity. The text lets us know where they are going because to walk north to a place like Caesarea of Philippi is intentional on Jesus' part as the rabbi of His beloved *disciples*. Also called Banias, this town is the Las Vegas of Israel. Controlled by the Romans and used as a leave of absence destination for Roman soldiers, Banias is a central hub for the worship of the god, Pan.

When you visit the ruins today you walk into a relatively small area spewing fresh water from Mount Hermon. At the center of your visual picture is a large cave that has been called the Gates of Hades since before the time of Christ. The pagans believed this to be the entrance to the underworld. Worshippers often threw animal and infant sacrifices into the cave to appease the gods of the underworld. The giant rock cliff housing the cave known as the Gates of Hades is called the "rock of the gods." In the enormous rock wall, and just to the right of the cave you will notice several niches dedicated to Pan and his cohort Echo. Below the niches two courts have been excavated. The first is the "goat court" where fertility rituals took place. The second is the court "of the goat dancers" where sexually erotic dances are offered to appease the gods. In these courts orgies, homosexual sex, bestiality, and erotic dancing were common practices of the pagans. This is the focal point of Caesarea of Philippi. If you are in the region of Caesarea of Philippi you can see these acts of worship from any vantage point. Understanding this helps us understand the passage a little better. Why would Jesus march His boys to the darkest place in Israel to teach them who He is and how He will build His church?

My goal is not to teach you the main point of this passage or to lead you in a complete study of Jesus' teaching here. There are many "take-aways" from this text but I see two that encourage me as a parent leading my children toward biblical purity in a terribly dark day. First, Jesus will build His church in the midst of a pervasive, sexually driven culture and second Jesus the King is greater than any cultural sin.

Realizing Jesus is the best teacher who has ever walked the planet and that rabbis are notorious for using location and visual backdrop as an important aspect of the lesson, I have to ask why Jesus takes them to Banias? When you understand the place it becomes like my taking my girls to Bourbon Street in New Orleans to teach them something very important to the Kingdom of God while they are observing perversion and atrocity, so they will never forget. Here are my favorite quotes of Jesus from the passage:

> *"And I tell you, you are Peter, and on this rock I will build my church, and the gates of hell* (Greek is "Gates of Hades") *shall not prevail against it."* (Matthew 16:18)

> *"For whoever is ashamed of me and of my words in this adulterous and sinful generation, of him will the Son of Man also be ashamed when he comes in the glory of his Father with the holy angels."* (Mark 8:38)

So here is the parent angle. I believe Jesus points to the rock behind Him as He is teaching His disciples. They are looking at the rock of the gods and the Gates of Hades and the associated paganism and perversion when Jesus says, *"And I tell you, you are Peter, and on this rock I will build my church and the gates of hell* (Greek is "Gates of Hades") *shall not prevail against it."* I think Jesus is saying that He will build His church on the rock of Peter's confession that Jesus is the Son of the Living God and Jesus is saying that He will build His church on the very rock of the gods in the very entrance to the gates of hell. He will build His church in the very face of utter perversion and paganism and He will prevail even in a wicked and adulterous generation. Jesus knew the odds we would face. So take heart parent. Leading your children to a life of biblical purity is not too difficult for Jesus the King. Abide in

Him and He will lead you as you guide them and protect them in such a horrendous mine field.

IDENTITY IN CHRIST

After Paul tells us to flee sexual immorality in 1 Corinthians 6:18, he takes a moment to remind us why. It is interesting that he does not list a host of sexually transmitted diseases or the emotional and spiritual consequences of sexual immorality. Instead he goes to the heart of the matter. This is much bigger than a moral issue for the apostle Paul. Instead he teaches to the heart. First Corinthians

> **Teaching to the heart means moving past behavior to the greater truth of identity in Christ.**

6:19-20 says, *"Or do you not know that your body is a temple of the Holy Spirit within you, whom you have from God? You are not your own, for you were bought with a price. So glorify God in your body."*

There are two ways to teach commitment to purity. As parents we can teach for moral behavior. Most parents would be happy if their teenagers just controlled themselves sexually. The best parenting teaches to the heart. In other words the desired outcome is not simply good moral choices but more so an adolescent heart that breaks over the same things that maim the heart of God. Teaching to the heart means moving past behavior to the greater truth of identity in Christ. The big questions our kids need to answer in their hearts are "Who am I?" and "Whose am I?" Information is a part of this but a greater part is a transformation of the heart orchestrated by the Holy Spirit.

Our children wrestle with God to answer these questions. We are here to help them in their wrestling. Remember we can guide them toward life in Christ but they choose to follow. So what should we do? We need to lead intentional Faith Talks around the core competency of identity in Christ. Every person makes decisions concerning life and behavior based on a personal clarity concerning identity in Christ. If you don't believe Christ is your King then you become your own master affording yourself the opportunity to define truth. If however you believe Jesus paid for your sin with His own sinless blood, redeeming you from your place of spiritual imprisonment and has ascended into heaven ruling at the right hand of the Father, likely you will view yourself as His possession. This choice to love Christ by submitting yourself to His Lordship means we have truth defined for us in the pages of God's Word. Understanding our identity in Christ means we long to live life according to His plan. Helping our children learn their true identity as one of God's kids is central to their ability to make a commitment to biblical purity and then live by it. There are many resources designed specifically to help you talk with your kids about their identity in Christ and how their moral behavior flows from that primary relationship with Jesus.[3] When it comes to identity in Christ the most powerful Faith Talk is the demonstration of your life as a Christ-follower.

BIBLICAL SEX

We are pretty much experts on telling our children what is wrong about sex. We should spend more time teaching them what is right about sex. The greatest thing you can do as a parent in the "sex" category is to reclaim sex in your family, changing it from a perverted bad word back into a beautiful and pleasure filled gift from the Lord. Here are some key principles to teach when having Faith Talks and capturing God moments with your teenager.

- **God's Design**—Sex is a creation of God himself. It is not bad but instead holy in the right context. Since God designed sex, it is best when it is practiced according to the Designers plan. Biblically, sex is reserved for a married husband and wife. Sex is for marriage alone because it fosters a deep connection physically, spiritually, and emotionally. Often Scripture uses the word "know" to describe a sexual encounter. Genesis 4:1 says, *"Now Adam knew Eve his wife, and she conceived and bore Cain…."* The word for "know" in Hebrew is *Yada*. It is the most intimate way to know someone. This kind of knowing is for one man and one woman for a lifetime or at least until death do us part. This intimacy yields an emotional connection that paves the way for the next generation. Procreation is God's plan to create new generations for His glory. Sex is a gift from God, not a dirty, hidden secret.

- **God Wants Us to Enjoy It**—God designed sex as a pleasure-filled experience both physically and emotionally. Sometimes our culture paints a picture of married sex as boring. In fact, married sex is the best kind of sex. There are countless studies revealing that married couples in a monogamous relationship are the most sexually satisfied people on the planet. Read the Song of Solomon, the most erotic book of the Bible. Tell me God doesn't want us to enjoy sex in the context of marriage. Whoa!

- **Sex Is Spiritual**—Genesis 2:18-25 shows us the first wedding ceremony in history. Verse 24 tells us that as they consecrate the marriage they become "one flesh." It is also true that their souls tie together. Sexual intercourse is spiritual and is either excellent or destructive. This spiritual bond is reserved for one man and one woman for a lifetime. Sex either brings glory to Jesus or defames His name. Sex is intrinsically spiritual and therefore must be exercised by the direction of the Holy Spirit alone. Anything outside of His design is damaging and hurtful.

YOUR ISSUES WITH SEX

Parents often superimpose personal issues with sex on the way we discuss and teach our children about sex. We have taught countless seminars on this subject at our church. We see everything from embarrassment and shame to disgust and anger when we equip parents to talk with their kids about sex. Some parents cannot imagine allowing sex to be an open topic for conversation in their home. That is because they view sex as dirty. We often view sex as dirty because we have sexual sin or sexual abuse and trauma in our past or present. In an effort to keep our children from experiencing the same thing we often duck the issue. This is the wrong approach. Instead, we should confess our sin and seek forgiveness from the God who wipes the slate clean when we ask Him to restore us completely. If we have abuse in our past we need to find freedom from the traumatic effects. This is not a lightweight parenting issue. We are talking about difficult work. If this is you, find a pastor or a Christian counselor and start the process of walking in freedom. Not only will you find peace, but you will stop the generational wounds related to sexual sin. Instead, you will pass a healthy view of sex on to the next generation. Help your kids commit to biblical purity by dealing with your own.

FAMILY CELEBRATION

Celebrating milestone 4 comes after the Faith Talks, God moments, and conversations necessary for your teenager to commit to biblical purity. The family celebration can be as simple as a gathering in your living room, backyard barbeque, or dinner at a favorite restaurant. Consider developing a family commitment to biblical purity that your teenager will sign as a part of a greater family celebration.

PURITY FOR LIFE PLEDGE[4]

→ MORAL EXCELLENCE ←

I recognize there is an absolute standard of right and wrong. While surveys indicate that the majority of my peers will make moral choices based on what "feels right at the time," I will make moral choices based on the standards set forth in God's Word, the Bible.

PURITY

I will not date anyone who is not a Christian. I will not engage in any activity that I would feel uncomfortable doing if Jesus Himself were visibly present. Should I find myself in a sexually tempting situation, I will flee immorality.

"Believing in Purity for Life, I make a commitment to God, myself, my family, my friends, my future mate, and my future children to a lifetime of purity including sexual abstinence from this day until the day I enter a biblical marriage relationship."

_____
Signature   Date

After the student signs the card pray a blessing over them and reassure them you will be there for them all along the way. Then present them with a purity ring as a symbol of their commitment to purity.

Often the local church offers a program through the youth ministry to help parents equip their children and celebrate a commitment to purity. This will be a valuable resource to you. "True Love Waits" is a movement around these milestone four issues. For even more assistance leading your children to commit to biblical purity visit www.truelovewaits.com. May the Lord bless you as you guide your children along this part of the legacy path.

MILESTONE 5: RITE OF PASSAGE

Two years or so will pass between milestone four and milestone five. In those years your middle school child will become a sophomore or junior in high school. For some kids this is the difference between gangly awkwardness and the appearance of manhood or womanhood. Many parents offer increasing freedom at this time in the form of expanding curfew and access to a car. This stage of life involves increasing freedoms. With freedom comes responsibility. How will we guide our teenagers to embrace biblical manhood or womanhood by the time they are sixteen? What constitutes for them a spiritual rite of passage into adulthood?

CORE COMPETENCIES

This is one of the most important treks along the milestone path. Take your time and do it right. Lead the Faith Talks and capture the God moments leading up to a very special rite of passage ceremony. Biblical training always precedes celebration. If you celebrate a milestone without equipping your child you are just throwing a party. Here are several core competencies we must teach our children as they begin their passage into adulthood.

BIBLICAL MANHOOD/WOMANHOOD

We live in a culture where boys do not think about becoming men until they are twenty-five. The Hebrew context of the Bible suggests boys become men by the age of thirteen and girls are confirmed as women by the age of twelve with the proper biblical training. We have lowered the bar in Western Christianity. Between eighth grade and tenth grade parents are to lead focused Faith Talks around the biblical roles of men and women.

Throughout Scripture God defines the roles of men and women according to His good design. As with all things, life works best when we do it the Designer's way. Leading your son or daughter well along this section of the path is critical to their developing biblical worldview. Evaluate the roles of men and women through the lens of Scripture and then teach it to them using Faith Talks, God moments, and most importantly the model of your own life and marriage. Here are some questions we need to answer for our children:

WHAT DOES A BIBLICAL MAN LOOK LIKE?

- He is a lover of God. (Deuteronomy 6:5 and Matthew 22:37)
- He is a lover of others. (Leviticus 19:18 and Matthew 22:39)
- He is loyal. (Hosea 6:6)
- He is a servant leader. (Matthew 20:26-27)
- He is kind, humble, and honest. (Ephesians 4:32, Philippians 2:3, Ephesians 4:25)
- He is self-disciplined. (1 Timothy 4:7-8)
- He is full of integrity. (Proverbs 10:9)
- He perseveres. (Galatians 6:9)

WHAT DOES A BIBLICAL WOMAN LOOK LIKE?

- She is a lover of God. (Deuteronomy 6:5 and Matthew 22:37)
- She is a lover of others. (Leviticus 19:18 and Matthew 22:39)
- She is noble and respected. (Proverbs 31:10, 25, 28)
- She is diligent. (Proverbs 31:13)
- She is an early riser and a provider. (Proverbs 31:14-15)
- She is a steward. (Proverbs 31:15-16)
- She is strong and persistent. (Proverbs 31:19, 25, 27)
- She is resourceful and hospitable. (Proverbs 31:18, 20, 21-22)
- She is confident. (Proverbs 31:18)
- She is happy and faithful. (Proverbs 31:25, 27, 30)
- She is blessed. (Proverbs 31:28-31)

WHAT ARE THE BIBLICAL ROLES OF MEN AND WOMEN?

As the Creator of the Universe, God needs no real resume or list of references to vouch for the fact that He knows what He is doing. Since He designed humanity, men, women, family, and marriage, He knows how it works best regardless of cultural context or time period. God clarifies the roles of women and men early in the Creation account. Genesis 2:15-18 tells us that Adam was placed in the Garden of Eden to "*work it and keep it.*" The Lord had compassion on Adam and said that it was not good for him to be alone. "*I will make him a helper fit for him.*" Simplistically, the whole counsel of Scripture teaches that men and women compliment each other well when they operate in their biblical roles. Helpers are not weak and protectors and providers are not dominant. Instead, together they bring unity and peace to family and life supporting each other as they live life in Christ. Preparing our children to understand their biblical role in God's design allows them to step into manhood or womanhood in a godly way.[5]

SPIRITUAL GIFTS AND SERVING

Part of exercising our faith as men and women is to recognize our spiritual gifts and use them as we serve Christ in the family, church, and the world. First Corinthians 12–14 lists spiritual gifts and the correct use of them in serving the body of Christ. Familiarize yourself with the list and ask yourself what you see your young Christ-follower utilizing naturally. What gifts and passions does your child possess that indicate the use of his gifts? Cultivate those gifts by serving together in your faith community. Your church likely offers opportunities to discover spiritual gifts. Partner with your church to discover these gifts and ways to use them in your local congregation. Serving together is the best model of using our gifts to build up the body of Christ.

BASIC TENETS OF THE FAITH

Between milestone four and milestone five use Faith Talks to teach the basic doctrines of the Christian faith. Our children need to understand the biblical foundation they stand on in order to pursue life in Christ as an adult. This idea simply horrifies many parents. At my church we try to give parents an easy way to correctly teach biblical doctrine in the context of Faith Talks. Utilizing John Piper's *Baptist Catechism*[6], you can lead two years of Faith Talks, one question at a time. The catechism provides a systematic approach to teaching doctrine and allows you as the parent to stay one question ahead. This gives you a win and allows for great conversation around the Scripture even if you struggle to know what doctrine to teach. Just stay one question ahead.

FAMILY CELEBRATION

Celebrating rite of passage is very special. The event is to be a memorable occasion where the student ceremonially passes into manhood or womanhood. Often the gathering includes people who have been instrumental in the child's spiritual development toward milestone five. Fathers lead the ceremony for their sons and mothers lead the ceremony for their daughters if the family structure allows. Every family chooses to design the ceremony according to their own style and budget. I have attended right of passage ceremonies in the backyard and I have attended them at the most expensive steak house in Houston. All were equally meaningful.

The ceremony consists of several sacred moments in which the parent reminds the young man or woman just what they have learned about biblical manhood or womanhood. Others are invited to speak into the young person's life in the form of verbal or written blessings. A video of pictures might be shown of the young man or woman illustrating the physical progression toward adulthood over the past sixteen years. Usually a meal is shared together. Finally a symbol and a blessing are given by the parent to the child now entering adulthood.

Rite of passage ceremonies are unique to each family and situation. Read as a friend of mine recounts his son's rite of passage ceremony:

> *My son's rite of passage was a defining moment for him. The night was a tangible and unforgettable time when the men closest to him would help him take the leap to manhood.*
>
> *We traveled one hour outside of our community to a Christian campground with a lake. Zach and I built a fire beside the lake and enjoyed about an hour together until sundown. As darkness fell, a vanload of my friends who had invested into Zach parked behind a barn. I then sent Zach up the hill to meet the first one. Each man stepped out of the barn with*

the same question for him, "Zach are you ready to become a man?" I had asked each man to speak to him about a quality that I had observed in them personally as men. These qualities were Loyalty, a Servant's heart, Integrity, Sexual Purity, Perseverance, Discipline, and Loving people with grace. They took a slow walk around the lake discussing that character trait and then joined me at the fire while Zach continued around the lake with each man.

When finished with the marathon of trips around the lake we all sat around the campfire. I then asked each man to affirm Zach in his walk with Christ. I wrapped up this portion by speaking blessing over my son and all that he meant to me. He and I had already discussed in our weekly breakfast time at Chick-fil-a what a biblical man looked like. He would reject passivity, lead courageously, and accept responsibility. Things we had learned from the book, "Raising a Modern Day Knight." I used the moment at hand to tell him that I could not have dreamed of a better son to have. I reminded him that as the only son in the Kennedy home he would carry on the family name but more importantly he would one day be a husband and father to pass along the name of the Jesus to the next generation. I then gave him a sword to remind him the rest of his life of what a man is built upon. It was actually a "sword of the Spirit." Also a Bible just like the one I preach out of every Sunday morning with a letter written in the front from his dad.

We concluded the night with a "manly" meal fit for carnivores at the local barbecue restaurant.

We laughed a lot that night. We cried some too. It was one of the best nights of our lives.

I am dreaming of a day that boys and girls are led into biblical adulthood by their parents in an intentional and compelling way. Imagine a new generation of women who love the Lord their God with all of their heart, mind, soul, and strength. Dream with me of a generation of young men who "man up" as Christ-followers by the age of sixteen. If you do your part and I do mine to guide our children we leave behind a spiritual legacy that demands a Christ-centered culture shift.

MILESTONE 6: HIGH SCHOOL GRADUATION

Selfishly, I can't even think of this day yet. When I do, I get weepy dreaming of my children launching into life outside the nest. At the same time our legacy path has its destination in Christ-centered life exhibiting a healthy measure of independence. As we lead them on the legacy path there comes a time to let them walk ahead as we let go and trust them to follow Christ. How do we get there?

CORE COMPETENCIES

Preparing them for life outside the nest is intentional. As with each milestone there are several core competencies we need to teach our teenagers and give them opportunity to practice before leaving home. We have about two years between rite of passage and high school graduation. In that time we need to lead Faith Talks discussing important issues like basic apologetics, dating and marriage, God's plan for me, person of influence, and practical life-skills. Often when I introduce this list to parents of older high school kids they quickly become overwhelmed. Let me break it down so that you can see with some work, every Christian parent can teach these key concepts.

Apologetics as a discipline is a defense of the Christian faith. We should all know why we believe what we believe but sadly many Christians have difficulty articulating their faith and defending it biblically. Questions like, "If God is so loving why do we have the horrifying problem of evil and suffering in the world?" horrifies the average parent. We need to get equipped ourselves. Fight the urge here to avoid the difficult questions of the faith because you don't know the answer. Struggle with these questions together in your living room before your teenager becomes a student in a university level philosophy class. So what do you do? Again go to the resources. One particular resource that is helpful to parents it *The Truth Project* produced by Focus on the Family and taught by Dr. Del Tackett.[7] This Christian worldview apologetics course comes in a DVD set that is worth a family purchase. Watch the DVD's with your teenagers as your weekly Faith Talk. Travel through the workbook together. In this way you can solidify the biblical worldview you have been working to build into your child as you walked the legacy path and you can effectively deal with the difficult questions.

Taking the time to reiterate that God has a plan for their life is important before they leave the nest. God's plan will effect decisions that include if or where they go to college, what they major in, what kind of profession or trade they pursue, and who they date and marry. Milestone six brings about natural questions from the Christian teenager's perspectives like, "What is God's will for my life?" We need to gladly help them to begin to seek God for the answer to this question. We also need to teach them they are salt and light wherever they go according to Matthew 5:13-16. God has called our Christ-following teenagers to become persons of influence as they leave home and pursue life in Christ in the world.

It is imperative that we teach our kids basic life skills before they graduate from high school and leave home. Does your graduating senior know how to wash clothes and cook a meal? Can he balance a checkbook and manage a credit card or debit card? Does he know how to change a flat tire? These are just some of the issues we need to address as we prepare them to leave home. The years between milestone five and milestone six are likely some of the busiest. Make sure you maximize the time to intentionally prepare your graduating senior to effectively live as a Christ-follower outside of the comforts of your home.

FAMILY CELEBRATION: THE BLESSING

Milestone six offers a ton of built-in family celebration opportunities around the event of high school graduation. Let me encourage you to capitalize on the momentum of this natural milestone by adding a formal blessing to the regular celebrations.

We are wired to receive our parent's blessing. Think about it? Did you receive your parent's blessing as you were leaving home? Some of us are not even sure. A cursory study of the Old Testament lends credence to the fact that children crave the blessing of their parents. As a pastor who has the opportunity to counsel adults regularly I want you to know something. Many thirty and forty year old adults feel like a twelve year old on the inside when they begin to talk about their relationship with their father and mother. Often the root of many of their issues relating to their own marriage and parenting centers around an emotional and spiritual chasm that should be filled with the blessing of their parents. The problem is parents often unintentionally neglect this important need in the lives of their children.

Milestone six is a perfect opportunity to write a blessing that your now adult child, can take with them as they leave home. As you prepare to write a blessing for them take some time to read the book, *The Blessing,* by John Trent and Gary Smalley. Arrange a special time to present your graduating senior with the blessing. Read it aloud to them and then present it to them assuring them that you believe God has great things in store for them. Do not underestimate the power of the blessing. It is in receiving their blessing that we give them the confidence they need to march into adulthood touting a biblical worldview in a world full of lies.

When I was writing my first book, *Shift: What it Takes to Finally Reach Families Today,* I solicited stories from parents and children who had been walking the path. More than any other milestone, the written blessings of milestone six came pouring in . . . but not from the parents. I received them from college students who are immensely proud of their parent's blessing. Here is a simple but meaningful example.

> *Dear Chad,*
>
> *You came into our lives as a blessing. Your entry on this earth was perfectly timed by God so that we received blessing and joy. We experienced new hope in you. We are so proud of you and how you work hard to excel at whatever task you pursue. We have faith that you are in God's hands and He will guide you in your choices regarding your future.*
>
> *This is our blessing for you:*
> *~ May you be a man who is strong in the Lord and in His mighty power. (Ephesians 6:10)*
> *~ May the Lord be your counselor all the days of your life. Even in the night, may the Lord instruct your heart. (Psalm 16)*
> *~ May your walk be blameless and your work be righteous,*
> *~ May the Lord keep your tongue from sin and your relationships pure.*
> *~ May you be honorable, loving and generous with your money.*
> *~ May the Lord keep you in His way so that you will not be shaken. (Psalm 15)*
> *~ May the God of hope fill you with all joy and peace. (Romans 15:13)*
> *~ May the Lord watch over your life and keep you from all harm. (Psalm 121:5)*

~ May the Lord bless you and make His name live on in you and in your children after you. (Genesis 48:16)

We love you,
Mom and Dad

MILESTONE 7: LIFE IN CHRIST

Milestone seven is the end goal of the legacy path but it is also the beginning of another journey. Milestone seven is an abiding relationship with Jesus Christ in adulthood. This milestone is the official end of your parenting your child while they are under your roof and the beginning of their spiritual walk with Christ as an adult. In this phase of life you become less of the lead guide on the legacy path and more of a wise counselor that your adult child can call on as they navigate Christ and the culture, leading others along the legacy path. This is also your personal journey with Christ. Though you are older and have walked the path before, you can always deepen in your relationship to Christ and the practical living out of your biblical worldview.

CORE COMPETENCIES

Where do you find core competencies for a life in Christ that work for every season of adulthood from younger to elder? The answer is in the gospels. If you study Matthew, Mark, Luke and John closely you will discover several lessons that Jesus teaches His disciples over and over again. Each lesson involves a characteristic of a life in Christ regardless of season of life. They include the importance of prayer and Scripture, an authentic faith, becoming an obedient follower, being a disciple-maker, giving and serving, and community with other Christians.

> You will discover that your life in Christ is the best teacher of the next generation.

You read a lot about milestone seven when you read about abiding in Christ. My question for you as a parent is this: do you demonstrate a milestone seven lifestyle each day? If we want our kids to be adults who live life in Christ then they must see it in you and me. How is your growing understanding and application of the Scripture? How is your prayer life? Do you follow Christ obediently? Are you making disciples by leading your children along the legacy path and helping others learn to do the same? Do you give and serve just as Christ gave and served? Do you have real community with others who offer biblical relationship? You will discover that your life in Christ is the best teacher of the next generation. Living it out in front of them every day—this is the way of the legacy path.

ENDNOTES

[1] http://www.cdc.gov/HealthyYouth/sexualbehaviors/index.htm, August 16, 2010.

[2] Ephesians 5:3–5.

[3] For an up-to-date list of milestone 4 resources visit www.legacymilestones.com/milestone4resources.

[4] Adapted from the "True Love Waits" pledge. www.truelovewaits.com.

[5] For more information and resources on biblical manhood and womanhood visit www.cbmw.org.

[6] Access this resource at www.desiringgod.org.

[7] www.thetruthproject.org.

Thoughts for Discussion with Your Spouse or Small Group

1. Where are your teenagers on the legacy path? What is the milestone you are leading them toward next?

2. How can you begin leading your teenagers spiritually if you have not been intentional at all to this point? How should you begin?

3. Have you taught your teenager the importance of biblical purity? What can you do in your home to open this conversation and equip them with truth?

4. How is your heart connection with your teenager? What can you do to improve that connection?

5. Pray for wisdom in leading your teenager spiritually especially if this is new to your family. Figure out where they are on the legacy path and begin to lead them. Make a list of things you need to do to get ready for the journey.

CHAPTER 7

CHURCH + HOME

I t is a humbling thought to meditate on God's design for spiritually training the next generation. Truly, as parents, we are called and designed to be the primary faith trainers of the children or teenagers growing up in our homes. God uniquely designed family to be the lead vehicle on the road to spiritual formation. As parents we do well to own our place of influence and maximize our spiritual leadership in the family.

Though we take the lead we are not alone on the legacy path. Let that thought soak in for a few seconds. The legacy path would be a miserable journey if we had to go it alone. God has given us a gift in the form of a faith community called the local church that partners with us all along the way as we lead our children spiritually. In a very real sense the partnership between family and church provides everything a child needs to develop in her faith as she travels through the spiritual milestones of life. Hold onto this. As a parent you are not alone.

> **In a very real sense the partnership between family and church provides everything a child needs to develop in her faith as she travels through the spiritual milestones of life.**

INSULA

First century Judaism teaches me lessons that infiltrate my 21st century understanding of the church and family. There is a place in the Galilee known as Chorazin. Unfortunately the little village is known for Jesus' famous line, "Woe to you Chorazin" found in Luke 10:13. A visit to Chorazin offers incredible insight into the lifestyle of the religious families that the writers of the gospels and Paul understood as they penned the biblical text. The dwelling places of families in Chorazin are characteristic of common people who lived in Galilee during Jesus' life and ministry on earth. The term most often used to describe the dwelling place is *insula*. The idea of an *insula* community is simple. *Insula* is a large rectangular courtyard surrounded on each side by small dwellings that look a lot like rooms. The rooms open into the courtyard providing a natural gathering place for play, conversation, and community. You can imagine how well the people living in *insula* get to know each other. They spend the days together working and the evenings together talking and serving one another. They are connected and turn to each other for advice. They are not isolated or alone but instead they dwell in community. They worship together in the synagogue and challenge each other daily to live according to the *Torah* or instructions that contain the very words of God. In a 1ˢᵗ Century community driven by Deuteronomy 6 people depended on each other for friendship, family support, and help. They walked the legacy path together, and naturally because of their attention to the Word of God and their community based context. I love the picture of *insula*.

Our situation is different. We are transient, independent, and isolated to a degree. You can live on a cul-de-sac with 20 other houses and not really know the people who live literally feet from where you sleep unless you are very intentional. In our context the culture is not so nicely founded in the Words of God. The people of our culture value individualism more highly than community. Yet God gives us the gift of the local church providing us the *insula* we need as we walk the legacy path.

When we realize the importance of others in our child's faith development we become better spiritual parents.

I love the culture of the early church described in Acts 2:42-47. The Scripture tells us that the people devoted themselves to learning the Bible, breaking bread together, and prayer. They had everything in common and if anyone of family was in need the others gave without hesitancy. They worshipped together regularly and the Lord brought others into their group who were also finding the answer to life in Jesus. This is exactly what the local church provides for us today. Even the best family leads better spiritually when they do it in partnership with their faith community. Today may be the day you encourage a family that is struggling to lead their children along the legacy path. Rest assured a day is coming when you will need similar support and encouragement. This is the beauty of authentic community realized in the local church. When we realize the importance of others in our child's faith development we become better spiritual parents.

> Even the best family leads better spiritually when they do it in partnership with their faith community.

EVERY CHRIST-FOLLOWER IS A DISCIPLE-MAKER

There is a reason Jesus commands every Christ-follower to make disciples in Matthew 28:18-20. In fact the disciples to whom He was speaking directly were likely not parents at the time Jesus issued the mission to go and make disciples. Jesus did not need to command parents to go and make disciples because that was a given in the context of a *Sh'ma* driven culture. When He involves every Christ-follower in the process of making disciples He is simply saying whether you are married, single, have kids, don't have kids, have grandchildren or don't, you are to make disciples. This mandate creates an intricate tapestry of others who can and will invest in the lives of our children spiritually. You will most often find those like-minded other Christ-followers in your local church.

Every child or teenager needs several people in his life to influence him spiritually. It is unmistakable biblically that the parent is to play the lead role in the faith formation of a child. Others however come alongside the parent as echoing voices in a partnership to guide the next generation along the legacy path. Who are the intentional others in the lives of your children? Might I suggest a few?

Children's pastors and youth pastors are keenly aware of the drastic need to partner with the family to equip the generations. They have read the studies; they have been to the conferences; and they have experienced ministry long enough to know that their ministry efforts in the life of a child are only as effective as their intentional partnership with the family. Get to know your kid's children's pastor or youth pastor. They are likely to be some of the best influences your child can have outside the family.

Our churches boast an army of volunteer disciple-makers eager to connect with your child and help him grow spiritually. Different churches have different ministry strategies but inevitably there is a volunteer leader teaching your child's Sunday School class or small group. Every week you attend church your child or teenager is being taught the Bible by someone. Get to know his Sunday School class teachers and small group leaders. Here's an idea. Have them over for dinner and get to know them as a family. Thank them for the time they invest and pursue a relationship with them. After all they are investing in your child at church like you are investing in them at home. These special people are going to partner with you to shape your child spiritually.

Extended family members can also serve as key partners in the effort to raise our children biblically. More and more grandparents are discovering ways to invest in their grandchildren spiritually. Count it a blessing if you live near relatives who follow Christ. Strategize with grandparents, aunts, uncles, and cousins, as you seek to develop a legacy of Christ-followers in the next generation of your family. Sometimes the greatest partners in discipleship are the very people that we gather with on special occasions like Thanksgiving and Christmas. If it is possible in your extended family, build partnerships with the people who love your kids almost as much as you do.

There is another group of people who will influence your children spiritually if you allow them. I call them "path people." They are the people whom the Lord puts in your path to bless you and your children relationally and spiritually. You have to watch for them. Sometimes they have no official capacity like Sunday School teacher or youth leader but they are solid Christ-followers as evidenced by their life, and they love you and your family. These "path people" have been invaluable to Angela and me as parents throughout the years, especially in situations that seem beyond our understanding or experience as we enter new stages of the legacy path. Watch for these people. They are a gift and likely will not stop investing in your child just because they move up a grade and are no longer in their Sunday School class or small group. These people may walk with you the whole way.

ECHOING VOICES

I have been coaching my kids' soccer teams for a number of seasons. At first they loved it. Then something happened. I noticed as they developed in their skill levels and confidence they also did not hear me as well. They would however receive practical instruction well from other coaches. The

> As parents we are wise to allow others to echo our voice.

same is true in my church. Sometimes people out of relational familiarity will not hear what I have to say as well as an outside consultant they have never met before. Potentially I could have offered the same counsel as the consultant but because he is an outside "expert" in his field, he is heard. I think it is funny that oftentimes the same message can be heard different ways simply because of who is communicating the message.

The same is true in spiritual parenting. When our children are young they hang on our every "Faith Talk" so to speak. When they get older and begin thinking for themselves it is helpful to have others perceived by our children as experts speaking the same message into their lives. As parents we are wise to allow others to echo our voice. Sometimes your child will not hear it from you, but the youth pastor may say the same thing and they hear it loud and clear. Maximize your *insula* with echoing voices.

DEMONSTRATED CHRISTIANITY

We are all different as followers of Jesus. We have different spiritual gifts, God-given talents, and abilities and unique passion areas. We have different personalities and experiences that lead us to practice the common and biblical disciplines of the faith in ways that are affected by our uniqueness. It is good for our children to observe Christianity demonstrated through other lives than just their parents.

When I was growing up my parents played an intentional and important role in my faith formation. I learned so much from their teaching and example. As a teenager I began to wonder how God wanted my understanding of the faith to chart the course for the rest of my life. As I looked at my godly parents, I could not see exercising my faith in exactly the same way they did. My dad was a businessman exercising his faith in the workplace. Honestly, the idea of sitting behind a desk, traveling, making money, and impacting people for Christ along the way did not resonate with me. I know now that had a lot to do with my particular spiritual gifts, my personality, and a calling on my life.

I did have a youth pastor in my life whose life looked more appealing because of the way God had, in His sovereignty designed me for a unique purpose in His kingdom. My relationship with my youth pastor allowed me to observe another godly man that demonstrated Christ in a different way than my own father. This model was healthy and helpful for me as I sought God for whom He wanted me to become. It was part of God's plan to use the biblical worldview I had gained from my parents and allow me to see that lived out in a different way through another life. For me this other relationship along the legacy path helped me discover how God might use me in ministry. Demonstrated faith in the lives of trusted others is an imperative aspect of the legacy path and crucial to your child's faith development.

YOU NEED OTHERS TOO . . .

Parenting is the most rewarding, joyful, and yet difficult, heartbreaking work. There will be times when you celebrate milestones with others from your church but there will also be times you need others to hold you up in the midst of heartbreak or disappointment. When you don't know where to go or what to do you will need others as a source of wise counsel. In short, you and I need community as much or more than our kids do.

Seriously, who are your people? You should not try and guide your children along the legacy path alone. Are you involved in a local church that teaches the Bible and offers opportunity for you to build your *insula*? At our church we ask our people if they have a 2:00 A.M. friend. Do you have people in your life you would be confident in calling at two in the morning if you were experiencing crisis? Do you have Christian friends who are walking the path as well? Who do you have coffee with or lunch with or some sort of ongoing conversation about Christ, life, and family? We need each other for the journey. Some say it takes a village. I say that it takes a church. Church plus home is a great partnership.

Thoughts for Discussion with Your Spouse or Small Group

1. Are you connected in a local church? If not make a list of churches you would like to visit. Make a plan for which one you will visit first and get there next Sunday.

2. Who is the children's pastor or youth pastor at your church? Do you know them well? If not, stop now and make a plan to get to know them. Have them over for dinner or take them to lunch after church one Sunday. (Pastors love that)

3. Who are the Sunday School teachers or small group leaders in your kid's life? What can you do to get to know them?

4. Who are the "path people" in your family's life? Pray and thank God for them. If you can't identify any, pray specifically that God would bring these people into your life soon.

5. Make a list of the top 5 influential people in your child's life other than you. Are they Christ-followers?

CHAPTER 8

WHAT IF IT DOESN'T WORK?

When I first started teaching the principles of the legacy path to people in my church some years ago most parents were ecstatic. They were so happy to have a plan for leading their children spiritually. There was however a reaction I did not anticipate, probably out of sheer ignorance or lack of life experience. The reaction came from empty-nesters who were grieving the spiritual life of their adult children. At first, I kind of blew this off thinking to myself, "Well, there is nothing we can do now except pray." That thought was insensitive, incorrect, and compassionless.

What began as a subtle reaction from a few became a ground swell of emotion among empty-nesters and senior adults. When I taught Scripture like 3 John 4, *"I have no greater joy than to hear that my children are walking in the truth,"* some of the empty-nester crowd would remind me that the inverse is also true. We have no greater sorrow than to hear that our children are not walking in the truth. Once I was teaching Proverbs 22:6, *"Train up a child in the way he should go; even when he is old he will not depart from it"* and a gentlemen literally shouted out, "Not always!" I was beginning to realize he was right.

Clearly many parents of adult children have pain associated with their prodigal children. I have listened to countless stories of parents who did everything right spiritually. They demonstrated the faith and led Faith Talks before they ever heard the words Faith Talk. They celebrated milestones before the path was mapped for them and they brought their kids to church in an intentional effort to partner with others who longed to invest in the next generation spiritually. As their children grew up they became adults who chose another path. I held an older man up recently as he wept over his homosexual son that once signed a biblical purity commitment. I listened to a friend as she and her husband waded through the treacherous waters of letting their young adult son walk off the path by his own volition. I know families that did it all right and yet their adult children choose a path that brings them to a place of spiritual insanity. They know the truth but they choose a lie. At this point I understand a very important principle. It could happen to any of us. We can do everything right and yet our children can choose lies over legacy for a season. What a horrifying thought and what an excruciatingly painful experience for some good parents! What if it doesn't work to have Faith Talks, capture God Moments, Celebrate Milestones, and demonstrate authentic faith?

PRODIGALS

There are no perfect parents. There are also no perfect children. The Scripture teaches us that in fact there are no perfect people. One day the Pharisees and the teachers of the law were grumbling about Jesus because He *"receives sinners and eats with them"* as recorded in Luke 15:2. In response to this religious criticism Jesus told three stories: the parable of the lost sheep, the parable of the lost coin, and the parable of the prodigal son. All of these stories carry a common theme: even regular people work to restore something precious that has been lost.

The parable of the prodigal son is the most crucial to the legacy path. You can read the entire parable in Luke 15:11-32. It is the story of a father with two sons. The eldest son is obedient and loyal but the youngest has a rebellious spirit. The parable begins as the younger son comes to the father and asks for his inheritance early so he might strike out on his own. The Scripture says he did just that and he squandered all his father had given him by living recklessly.

Before we go on there are a couple of teaching points we need to consider. First in the Eastern context of the parable, it is completely disgraceful for a son to ask his father for inheritance prior to death. It is another slap in the face for the son to take the inheritance his father has worked to build, leaving home with it instead of remaining in the community of family and adding to the family business. Remember, this is not a Western son and father. The value in the first century Eastern context is loyalty to family and community in family. It would be rare for a young man to leave his family to live in another place. Interestingly, the father in the story does not argue with the son but instead freely gives the portion of the inheritance that is designated to him. My question is why?

THE QUANDARY OF FREE WILL

There are many different ways to look at the parable of the prodigal son. One way is to study it from the perspective of the father. The father in the story represents our Father. We learn something about God and how He parents His children in this parable. In His sovereignty God has given each of us a free will. He allows us to choose to love Him and walk in His way, and He allows us to choose another path. He gave us free will because He loves us and wants us to choose to love Him. Why does the father give his son the freedom to "take the money and run"? He does it because he loves him and in that gives him the freedom to choose his own path at the end of the day. God does the same thing with us. Think about your own life for a minute. God allows you to choose disobedience. This has some ramifications on parenting. Our children grow up to be adults who have been granted a free will. We can work hard to train them in the way they should go but there may be seasons of reckless living that are extremely painful. It is a reality by design. It is a real quandary. Free will means our kids may choose another way of living as adults apart from Christ, despite our best efforts. Take heart Mom and Dad; the story has just begun.

FREE WILL AND CONSEQUENCES

The parable continues as the young man squanders his wealth in a far away land and discovers the realities of financial ruin. In a last ditch effort to salvage his life he hires himself out to one of the citizens of that country who sends him into the field to feed the pigs. The young man finds himself so physically hungry that he longed to eat the same food that the pigs were eating.

We can infer that this is a Jewish father and son because of the original recipients of Jesus' parable, the Pharisees and scribes. When the Bible (Luke 15:13) says that the young man went to a far off land it describes for the hearer a journey from a *Torah* based, godly society to one of paganism. In Jewish life of the first century there were not many things more unclean than pigs. You would not have discovered pigs in the fields of *Torah* observant Jews.

Here we find our prodigal facing the consequences of leaving his father and sinfully squandering his wealth in reckless living (Luke 15:14-16). The young man in this parable is a boy that grew up in the culture that is most conducive to the *Sh'ma* of Deuteronomy 6:4-9. His father would have naturally taught him the Scriptures, taken him to Synagogue, celebrated the required feasts of Judaism, all to teach him the ways of God. Yet the son is now a best friend with the most unclean animal in the Hebrew Bible. The son is envious of the pig's food. He is hungry, alone, and miserable in a distant land. These are the consequences of his choices. God disciplines His kids and He often does it by teaching us in the midst of consequences resulting from our rebellious acts of free will.

I have counseled many parents who find their children in the midst of terrible consequences associated with their rebellious choices. The question I most often get from parents of prodigals is, "Do I bail them out or do I let them experience the consequences of their chosen path?" I will be honest. It is easy for me to give advice not yet knowing what it would feel like to have one of my own children eating with the pigs. At the same time I have been in ministry long enough to see different scenarios play out. I have learned in observation that parents who continually attempt to erase the consequences interrupt God's process of discipline causing their kids to return to their own vomit later. Parents who allow their prodigals to face the consequences of their own choices are more likely to witness true repentance and a return to God's way of living. Though consequences feel bad God uses them as a catalyst for repentance in prodigal children. My counsel is to allow your children to face the consequences of their chosen lifestyle all the while praying your guts out for their return. Fight for them in prayer!

T'SHUVA

Luke 15:17–19 tells us that in the midst of consequence the young man *"came to himself."* I believe this is the wisdom of Proverbs 22:6 in action. Though he became prodigal and experienced terrible discipline, there was a day when he remembered who he was and what it was like to live under the protection of his father. In the end he did not depart from his father's training. As the young man thought about his father's house he realized that even the servants never hungered because they were under the care of his father. He decided to go to his father. Very simply he arose and went. He knew the truth in his heart and what he must convey to his father according to Luke15:18. *"Father, I have sinned against heaven and before you."*

In Hebrew there is a word to describe this kind of intentional change of direction in life. It is the world, *T'shuva*. The word literally means to turn. It is the word that we translate as repentance. A prodigal finds his way back to the legacy path in true repentance. If we teach our children anything when they are young we must teach and model a repentant heart. The only hope for a destructive free will is a heart that repents.

I have a friend that comes to mind when I think about this situation. If I could tell her anything it would be to hope in the very Words of God. Though she has a prodigal son, she invested the Word in him while he was young. I believe one day, when he comes to himself, his heart will be drawn back to the very Words of his Father. I think he will repent and run back to his parents and his Father's way of living.

This, by the way, is why we cannot use the example of a parent who did everything right yet has a prodigal, as an excuse to throw out our responsibility to guide our children spiritually. The wisdom of Proverbs 22:6 prevails. *"Train up a child in the way he should go; even when he is old he will not depart from it."* Our prodigals will actually need our Faith Talks, God moments, milestones, and model when they finally realize they are eating with the pigs. Teaching a child about repentance and forgiveness may serve her well if she hits bottom as an adult. Repentance will be her way out.

THE GRACE OF THE FATHER

As the young man returned home his father saw him coming. The Scripture says, *"But while he was still a long way off, his father saw him and felt compassion, and ran and embraced him and kissed him* (Luke 15:20). The young man embraced his father humbly confessing his sin and admitting he was not worthy to be called son. Instead he would like to be a servant. His father calls for the best robe, and the family ring, and shoes. Then he throws a party celebrating his son's return. This illustrates some things.

God is a Father who longs for us to return. He is waiting for us eagerly, and when we return with a repentant heart He lavishes us with His grace. I am so glad because I have been that prodigal spiritually on so many occasions, and so have you. In a passage predicting the coming Messiah, Isaiah says, "*All we like sheep have gone astray; we have turned—every one—to his own way, and the Lord has laid on him* (Jesus) *the iniquity of us all*" (Isaiah 53:6). Romans 3:23–24 says it this way, "*For all have sinned and fall short of the glory of God, and are justified by his grace as a gift, through the redemption that is in Jesus Christ.*" The Father has been compassionate and graceful with us. He will be to our prodigal children as well when they *t'shuva*. As parents we are to eagerly anticipate the return of our prodigals. When they return we offer grace.

The hardest part is standing on that front porch waiting for their return. What do you do while you are waiting for them come home? Biblical parenting expert, Dr. Rob Rienow suggests that it is never too late to parent your prodigal children. Do you hear that? It doesn't matter if you are 80 and your child is 55! This is a great hope for all parents of adult children who have walked away from the faith. In his book, *When They Turn Away*, Rienow offers four steps every parent should take as they seek to lead their children back to a biblical faith.

1. Offer your heart to the Lord.
2. Turn your heart to your child.
3. Draw your child's heart to yours.
4. Point your child's heart to Christ.[1]

These steps may seem overly simplistic at first glance, but they represent a biblical proven strategy for parenting children who turn away from the faith. We see the father in the parable of the prodigal son take similar steps. The father must have offered his heart to the Lord as he grieved the departure of his son from his home and from the faith. The father's heart is turned toward the child as he eagerly awaits his return. We see this evidenced in the simple fact that the father is searching the horizon when his son returns. The father draws his child's heart toward his own as he pours out compassion and grace restoring his son to his proper place relationally. When we offer such compassion to our children in just the right moments, we point their hearts to Jesus. Our parental grace is a gateway back to biblical faith. When they finally humble themselves we turn them back to Christ and back to the legacy path. It really is never too late!

ALLOW YOURSELF GRACE

When it seemingly doesn't work, allow yourself some grace. There is a balance here. There is truth to the adage, "The apple does not fall far from the tree." If you recognize that your own sinful patterns have impressed your children in a negative way repent and seek God's forgiveness and seek your child's forgiveness. At the same time understand it is not necessarily your fault that your adult child becomes prodigal. Lay aside false guilt that will cause emotional and spiritual sickness. I know too many parents walking around with guilt that becomes spiritual bondage. Take a cross trip. Go to the cross of Jesus and lay down your guilt and receive His grace and hope. Your child is more His than yours. You are not the only one eagerly awaiting your child's return to the faith. The Father longs for your prodigal to come home. Hope in the Sovereign love of God for the life and soul of your child. The Faith Talks, God moments, and milestones will matter when your child finally *"comes to himself"* and starts the repentant journey home. Remember those disciples who quickly abandoned Jesus. They changed the world! God can do amazing things with His kids who once ate with the pigs. *"For this my son was dead, and is alive again; he was lost, and is now found. And they began to celebrate"* (Luke 15:24).

ENDNOTES

[1]Rob Rienow, *When They Turn Away: Drawing Your Adult Child Back to Christ* (Grand Rapids: Kregel Publications, 2010. 46-47).

Thoughts for Discussion with Your Spouse or Small Group

1. Do you know a family that seemingly did everything right and yet their adult child is spiritually A.W.O.L.? Stop now and pray for them.

2. What are your greatest fears associated with leading your children spiritually?

3. After reading this chapter, what might you change about the way you are parenting?

4. Has there been a time in your life when you were a prodigal? How did your parents respond? What did they do right and what did they do wrong? How did God respond?

5. In what ways do you need to learn to show compassion and grace?

CHAPTER 9

BIBLICAL PARENTING REQUIRES COURAGE

"When the Philistine arose and came and drew near to meet David, David ran quickly toward the battle line to meet the Philistine. And David put his hand in his bag and took out a stone and slung it and struck the Philistine on his forehead. The stone sank into his forehead and he fell on his face to the ground" (1 Samuel 17:48–49).

Intentional biblical parenting is not for the faint of heart especially when we live in a 21st century secular culture shaped largely by humanism and paganism. When we think of the influences that could possible creep into the lives of our children we often shudder. Technology, friends, state-mandated curriculum, media, savvy marketing, and pagan philosophies compete for the minds and souls of our children. It is our job to navigate the battlefield by leading them along the legacy path.

We face a very real enemy. The Bible calls him Satan. He despises God and His kids. Think about this. The Scripture teaches in Genesis 1:27 that God created men and women in His own image. When Satan sees us he sees the image of God. The enemy's personal vendetta is to kill, steal, and destroy the beautiful image of God according to John 10:10. Intentional spiritual parenting is spitting in the face of the enemy as you follow God and lead your children to do the same. The enemy will certainly fight back like a mighty giant that seems undefeatable. Some days you will find the spiritual battle raging in a powerful effort to steal the life of your child. On these days you and I need courage that comes from trust in God who is more powerful than the enemy. Courage is an interesting concept. Where does it come from and how do we get it? The Bible teaches that courage stems from faith in the God who is victorious no matter how fearful the circumstances appear. Courage also develops as we are obedient to walk in God's ways even in the face of adversity. Consider the case of a young shepherd named David in 1 Samuel 17.

ELAH VALLEY, ISRAEL CIRCA 1020 B.C.

The Scripture tells us that a battle was brewing once again between the people of Israel and the Philistines. The Philistines occupied the coastal plain of Israel closest to the Mediterranean Sea. The Israelites lived in the Judah Mountains seeking the protection of higher ground and rocky hiding places. For years these two people groups battled toe to toe often clashing in the *Shephelah*, or foothills, of Central Israel.

It is really no wonder they clashed. The two groups were simply so very different. They lived life through the filters of radically different worldviews. The Philistines were people of great size in comparison to the Israelites. They worshiped multiple foreign gods epitomizing paganism. They had the best technology life in those days had to offer. They stood in anger against the God of Israel and His people. The Israelites, on the other hand, were *Torah*-driven God-followers. They were on the legacy path. Of course, they followed better in some generations than others as you read in Psalm 78, but nonetheless they represented the worldview of God.

Whenever they fought, the Philistines traveled east from the sea and the Israelites traveled west from the mountains. They met in the fertile valleys and foothills of the *Shephelah*. This area of Israel was and is some of the most fertile ground in the world. It was a very strategic piece of land because of the trade route passing through it called the Via Maris opening trade from Egypt through Israel to Damascus. Whoever controlled the *Shephelah* influenced, and in a way, controlled the world. The *Shephelah* has always been a battleground and according to the Scripture it will be until the end. To a Jewish mind, the *Shephelah* is the place where worldviews collide. In those days it was the God-honoring worldview of the Israelites colliding with the pagan view of the Philistines.

On this day a young shepherd named David traveled from his hometown of Bethlehem to the front lines of battle in the valley of

Elah to determine the wellbeing of his older brothers at the request of his father Jesse. Being the youngest of all of Jesse's sons required David to stay home and tend the sheep instead of marching off to war with the rest of his brothers. Today he would leave the sheep behind, in good hands of course, and journey toward the excitement of battle. Arriving at Azekah in the Judah Mountains, David looked across the valley of Elah and observed the great Philistine encampment at Ephes Dammim near Socoh. There was a real sense of fear among the Israelite soldiers. A Philistine champion named Goliath stepped out into the valley each day and mocked the army of God as weak and insignificant. That is often the opposing worldview's favorite strategy against a biblical faith. Goliath stood over nine feet tall according to Scripture. Day after day, relentlessly, Goliath stepped into the valley and in a monstrous tone shouted words of challenge to the people of God. The challenge was simple and straight-forward. Choose a warrior, a champion of sorts, to fight Goliath one-on-one in the valley. Winner takes all. If the Israelite champion killed Goliath, all of the Philistine army would stand down and become servants of the people of Israel. If however, Goliath killed the Israelite in the valley, the people of Israel would become servants of the Philistines. Goliath issued this daunting challenge every day for forty days.

On hearing Goliath's words, King Saul and all the Israelites were dismayed and terrified. Interesting. King Saul, chosen by the elders of Israel to be king because he was the tallest man in Israel (1 Samuel 9:2), was shaking in his boots. I would say shaking in his armor, but apparently he did not even have the courage or the faith to put it on. Never choose a king for his height. As a man towering at 5' 7 1/2" on a good day, I like the way the rest of this story goes.

David enters the scene smelling the fear of his people in the air. His brothers were dismayed and terrified along with all of the other warriors of Israel. David heard the challenge of Goliath and watched as the armies of Israel trembled in great fear. In the midst of the fear, chaos, and confusion, David asked a very poignant and probably humiliating question as his brothers and the armies of Israel ran to hide in the cisterns of Azekah. *"Who is this uncircumcised Philistine, that he should defy the armies of the living God?"* (1 Samuel 17:26).

It seems odd that no one except a young shepherd considered the God factor in the equation. The word "Israel" can be translated "God prevails." So, no one in the army of "God prevails" even thought to consider that God might just be capable enough to handle this ostentatious giant.

David's brother Eliab burned with anger at David's statement. Eliab felt this way partly because of his own lack of courage and partly because his little brother seemed arrogant in a hopeless situation. He interpreted David's confidence in the Lord as conceit and wickedness. Sometimes people who exercise faith in courageous ways are viewed by others as arrogant and intolerant. Eliab demanded that David go back to the outskirts of Bethlehem and tend the sheep he left behind with a substitute shepherd.

David was relentless in the situation. He was simply wondering why no one would exercise the faith in God they so often boasted. Obviously everyone from King Saul down the ranks to the smallest peon in the Israelite army believed in his fear that Goliath was greater than God.

We are no different. We sometimes believe our own cultural obstacles are too great to challenge. We secretly believe our churches and our families are no match for the culture. We think the demise of the family in America is a ramification of the culture that cannot be avoided. We shake our heads in confusion believing there is really nothing we can do. We focus on making our family the best it can be without ever engaging the giant of the culture. In short, we fear the Western, humanistic, post-Christian culture of the 21st century. We are very close to losing in the *Shephelah* because we do not engage the giant in the place where worldviews collide the most: home.

Many Christian parents quietly think they cannot measure up against the prevalent mainstream thought of the day. They believe it impossible to stand against the pressure of what other parents allow their kids to do. Parents operate as if it is unrealistic to be completely Christian in this affluent, competitive, tolerant culture. Christian parents cower, feeling powerless against a persistent giant challenging them constantly. Christian parents forget about the God factor and neglect to faithfully apply the power of God in the context of their own home. Instead of fighting the giant, as Christian parents, we sometimes cower.

Not so with David. The shepherd made enough noise that day to gain an audience with King Saul. He convinced Saul to let him fight as Israel's champion against the pagan giant. Not bad for a shepherd too young to go to war. Saul put his best armor on David but it was uncomfortable and cumbersome. Leaving behind the armor of the King, David went to a small creek that runs through the valley of Elah. He chose five smooth stones and placed them in his shepherd's bag. Armed with a sling and stones David approached the giant in the *Shephelah* . . . the place where worldviews collide. He did not wait on the giant to move his direction; he confidently approached the giant. The Bible tells us that Goliath was both angry and insulted when he realized David was a young and inexperienced fighter. Goliath pronounced a curse by his gods upon the pathetic nature of his opponent. So here in the *Shephelah*, we have a showdown of biblical proportions . . . a nine-foot giant who is cursing by his gods versus a young shepherd armed only with a sling, five stones, and an enviable faith in God. Quite a drama!

Goliath announced that his plans were to give David's flesh to the birds of the air and the beasts of the field. In Goliath's view, this contest was over before it started. Goliath saw David as just a boy with sticks and stones. God had a very different view of course. The view from heaven saw a boy becoming a king.

Let us pause for a moment and check David's motive in this scenario. Was he in this battle for free publicity? Was he doing it for some kind of material reward? Was he fighting to receive personal glory? Was this a crafty political move by a very smart shepherd who originally entered the scene to bring his brothers lunch from home? No way! This was just a boy viewing his God as capable and acting in faith. The manifestation was an incredible act of courage that would change the course of a nation. The foundation is practical obedience and faith in God.

The Scripture teaches in 1 Samuel 17:46 that David answered Goliath's cursing with a statement of his own. *"This day the Lord will deliver you into my hand, and I will strike you down and cut off your head. And I will give the dead bodies of the host of the Philistines this day to the birds of the air and to wild beasts of the earth, that all the earth may know that there is a God in Israel."*

What is the motive? So the whole world would learn, in the place where worldviews collide, that there is a God! So David threw his rock and he killed Goliath. The dead bodies of the Philistine army were scattered along the road from Gath (Goliath's home town) to Ekron. On that day the whole world learned of the powerful God of Israel who is victorious in the place where worldviews collide over seemingly undefeatable enemies of opposing perspectives. David, the shepherd, exercised amazing courage because of his solid foundation of faith in God. He was on his way to becoming a man after God's own heart and King of Israel.

When we view God as capable we can act in faith in the midst of terrible circumstances. We are in a battle, you and I. The battle is a fight to redesign American culture in a God-honoring way by parenting the next generation. The battlefield is a *Shephelah* of sorts. It is the place where worldviews collide in our culture. It is the family and it appears that Christianity is losing on that front. Winning the battle will mean raising godly children who live life according to the worldview of the Bible. It means the church must partner with parents to equip the next generation. It means trusting God as we discover intentional spiritual parenting. It may seem different or more difficult but a change is necessary. We must parent with the courage of David as we lead our children on a path to biblical legacy.

FINAL THOUGHTS

It is humbling to think God chose us for this time in world history to parent the next generation of Christ-followers. We do it for two reasons. First because we love our children and we want God's best for them. Second, because biblical parenting has multi-generational ramifications. When you and I walk the legacy path we hurl a biblical faith into the generations. Not only will our parenting show the whole world there is one true God in our generation, but it will cause our children to lead their kids on the legacy path as well. A day is coming soon when new parents won't need to discover intentional spiritual parenting. Do you know why? The younger generation will know the path because they walked it with you as their guide. They will intentionally lead your grandkids spiritually and on and on it goes. Legacy is a beautiful thing. When you and I are with our Father in heaven, the generations on earth will continue to be impacted by our courageous guidance of our children along the legacy path. In this the whole world will know throughout the generations, Jesus is the Messiah and the King. This is the great hope for our children and for future generations. You have been chosen to play a lead role in the story. I pray that God will grant you wisdom, courage, love, compassion, grace, forgiveness, humility, and whatever else you need as you lead the next generation spiritually. There is a growing army of parents just like you and me seeking God for the faith of our children. Now we have a plan. Once the prophet Nehemiah faced an incredible challenge to rebuild Jerusalem in the face of a real and dangerous enemy. As he persuaded his people to engage in the battle he said these words as recorded in Nehemiah 4:14. "*Do not be afraid of them. Remember the Lord, who is great and awesome, and fight for your brothers, your sons, your daughters, your wives, and your homes.*" See you on the legacy path.

Thoughts for Discussion with Your Spouse or Small Group

1. What about the culture your family lives in competes with you as the primary faith influencer for your child?

2. How can you lead intentionally to overcome opposing outside influences?

3. After reading this book, how will you change the way you are spiritually leading your children?

4. When you think of the spiritual legacy you will leave behind for the generations, what are your hopes and dreams? What would you have to do to see those dreams come to fruition?

ABOUT THE AUTHOR

Brian considers his most important ministry as loving and serving his wife Angela and together parenting their children, Hailey, Madelyn, and Eden. He is the creator of the Legacy Milestones strategy designed to help the church and family work together to equip the next generation. Brian is the Author of the book *SHIFT: What It Takes to Finally Reach Families Today* as well as a contributor to several other books and resources. Brian served for 15 years in three churches as a student pastor and associate pastor including Kingsland Baptist Church in Katy, Texas. He now serves as Lead Pastor at Bay Area First Baptist Church in League City, Texas. Brian holds an undergraduate degree from Baylor University, a master's degree from Southwestern Baptist Theological Seminary, and a Doctor of Ministry degree from Liberty Baptist Theological Seminary for his work in family ministry and discipleship.

ALSO AVAILABLE
FROM BRIAN HAYNES

SHIFT: What it Takes to Finally Reach Families Today,
Group Publishing 2009

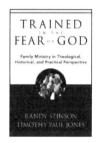

Family Faith Celebrations,
Group Publishing, 2010

Trained in the Fear of God,
Edited by Dr. Timothy Jones,
Kregel, 2011

LEGACY
MILESTONES

Visit Brian at **www.legacymilestones.com**

Family Ministry STARTS HERE